DATE			

THE REALITY OF NUMBERS

The Reality of Numbers

A Physicalist's Philosophy
of Mathematics

JOHN BIGELOW

CLARENDON PRESS · OXFORD
1988

Oxford University Press, Walton Street, Oxford OX2 6DP
Oxford New York Toronto
Delhi Bombay Calcutta Madras Karachi
Petaling Jaya Singapore Hong Kong Tokyo
Nairobi Dar es Salaam Cape Town
Melbourne Auckland
and associated companies in
Berlin Ibadan

Oxford is a trade mark of Oxford University Press

Published in the United States
by Oxford University Press, New York

British Library Cataloguing in Publication Data
Bigelow, John
The reality of numbers: a physicalist's
philosophy of mathematics.
1. Mathematics——Philosophy
I. Title
510'.1   QA8.4
ISBN 0–19–824957–8

Library of Congress Cataloging in Publication Data
Bigelow, John, 1948–
The reality of numbers.
Bibliography: p.   Includes index.
1. Mathematics—Philosophy. 2. Set theory.
3. Logic, Symbolic and mathematical.   I. Title.
QA8.4.B53 1988   510'.1   87–31454
ISBN 0–19–824957–8

Set by Wyvern Typesetting Ltd, Bristol
Printed in Great Britain
at the University Printing House, Oxford
by David Stanford
Printer to the University

Acknowledgements

Victoria University of Wellington, New Zealand, had an extraordinarily productive interaction between mathematicians and philosophers during the time I spent there, 1973–8, on the first lectureship of my academic career. I particularly remember the weekly seminars, including George Hughes and Max Cresswell from the philosophy department, and Wilf Malcolm, Ken Pledger, Rob Goldblatt, and others from the pure mathematics department. I also recall attending a superb course of lectures, given by Ken Pledger, on the history of mathematics.

I am also grateful to the philosophical community in New Zealand as a whole, both for the time when I was in New Zealand, and for the continued contact I have had by attending their annual philosophy conferences, and reading several papers there which evolved into this book. And long before my philosophical career, I was deeply influenced by a gifted musician and mathematics teacher in Christchurch, Kit Powell, a Pythagorean who enabled me to see the mathematics in music, and to hear the music in mathematics.

In Melbourne, I have tried out the ideas in this book at Melbourne University, Monash University, and (my own) La Trobe University. I have relied heavily on regular meetings of the Melbourne Semantics Group. Some of the local sources for my ideas are sufficiently acknowledged in the text. But one source is mentioned nowhere in particular, because it has contributed everywhere: and that source has been my colleague Robert Pargetter, with whom I have shared most of the courses I have taught at La Trobe University.

I began this book while on an Outside Studies Programme, from July 1983 to January 1984, granted by La Trobe University. In July I visited the Australian National University in Canberra, Sydney University, and the University of Wollongong, where I tried out some of the ideas which grew into this book. I have been particularly influenced by David Armstrong, both in discussions and in correspondence, and by my colleague Robert Pargetter.

From August 1983 to January 1984 I was in America; and I thank my family, Liz, Stephen, and Ben, for being with me in America while I worked on this book. (Thanks also to Stephen for the title.). I visited Syracuse University to see my former teacher, Jonathan Bennett; and

I am grateful to the whole department there for a very friendly and profitable visit. The remainder of my time in America was spent mainly at Princeton University. There, I attended lectures on quantum mechanics by K. de Conte; and this had a large effect on me, some of which has crept into the book. I was also influenced by discussions with Terry Tomkow, David Lewis, Mark Johnston, John Burgess, Douglas Jesseph, Paul Benacerraf, Bas van Fraassen, Saul Kripke, and other students, staff, and visitors there. And I am especially grateful to Douglas Jesseph for the assistance he provided, both during my stay and after I left, in translating for me all the previously untranslated portions of Frege's *Grundgesetze*.

J. B.

La Trobe University
August 1987

Contents

CONTENTS

III(b) *Wholes and Parts*

III(c) *Anyhow to Something*

Introduction

UNDER the shadow of logical positivism, it has been difficult to discuss metaphysics openly. And yet, important metaphysical opinions have stayed very much alive, often disguised as facts of language which native speakers can know simply in virtue of knowing their own language. Covertly, the metaphysical doctrine of *nominalism* has held ascendancy, more or less unchallenged, perhaps in part because as a negative doctrine it seems much less 'metaphysical' than its rival, *Platonism*. This has been a disaster for our understanding of mathematics.

Recently, metaphysics has been making something of a come-back. Nominalism is being challenged by Platonism and other kindred doctrines. This promises to cast new light on mathematics. In this book, I apply a realist theory of universals to the problem of understanding the nature of mathematics.

The kind of realism I advocate is a descendant of David Armstrong's a posteriori realism. This theory is distinguished from traditional Platonism in a variety of ways. To keep your bearings, you should remember that Armstrong was a founding architect of modern materialism. He will have no truck with transcendent Platonic Forms, and nor will I. Everything there is is *physical*—and this is worth saying, even though the term 'physical' sinks under scrutiny into a swamp of ambiguities. Hence universals, too, are physical. That is to say, the universals which exist are all real physical properties and relations among physical things. And thus, their existence cannot be deduced a priori, or founded simply on reflection about 'what every speaker knows'. Their existence is to be established by general scientific method—whatever that is. That is why Armstrong's view is called a posteriori realism.

Thus, I argue that the world around us, the world of space and time, does contain mathematical objects like numbers. I portray these as no mere abstractions, existing separately from the physical things around us. Nor do I portray them as mere ideas in the mind; nor as empty symbols which refer to nothing beyond themselves.

Plato was right in thinking that true knowledge concerns the things studied in mathematics. And Aristotle was right in thinking that true knowledge concerns the physical world around us. But they were both wrong in assuming that the things studied in mathematics are too pure and perfect to be found in the physical world we feel and smell around us.

I think of this book as Pythagorean in spirit, in the sense in which Galileo was a Pythagorean. If the rise of science in sixteenth- and seventeenth-century Europe was anything more than a continuation of ancient Greek science, if there was anything distinctive about the science of heroic figures like Copernicus, Galileo, Kepler, and Newton, it was a Pythagorean confidence that the physical world is laden with mathematical properties and relations.

If it is often hard to see clear and precise mathematical properties around us, this is only because there are so many of them, overlaid upon one another. By controlled experiments, each of these superimposed mathematical patterns can be separately displayed. In the sort of experimentation distinctive of modern science, sensory observation is important, but it is only productive when it has been tailored to reveal mathematical patterns. It is worth noticing that one of the earliest appearances of scientific experimentation was in the Pythagorean discovery of the mathematical proportions which underlie musical harmonies. Science has always been at its best when it has retained this blend of mathematics, manipulation, observation, and emotional response. This is because mathematical properties and relations are really there in the world, if only we can manipulate things in such a way as to make them emerge. And since we are physical beings ourselves, through and through, the same mathematical patterns that are in the world around us are also present inside us. That is why nature can be understood; and it is why there are deep affinities between aesthetic response and the perception of mathematical patterns.

My kind of Pythagoreanism is related to a current position in the philosophy of mathematics, called *structuralism*. The guiding idea of structuralism is that the subject-matter of mathematics does not consist in the various *things* which display various structures, but rather, the structures themselves which those things display. As Poincaré said in *Science and Hypothesis* (1905, p. 20):

Mathematicians do not study objects, but the relations between objects; to them it is a matter of indifference if these objects are replaced by others, provided that the relations do not change. Matter does not engage their attention, they are interested in form alone.

Most structuralists, however, are extremely coy about the status of 'structures'. Either they are closet nominalists, or else they at least take care to avoid saying anything positive about what exactly a 'structure' is. What distinguishes my theory is that I identify structures unambiguously with universals—properties and relations—and I do not scruple to grant them 'existence'. When two collections of individuals have the same structure, then I say that *there is* something which they have in common. We can refer to what they have in common; it can become a subject-matter for investigation. The structure is just as real as the things which have it.

Thus in an obvious sense, the brand of Platonism I advocate is a form of *realism*. The realism I advocate is the theory that there are universals, and that numbers in particular, and mathematical objects in general, are universals. I intend this existential claim to be understood in the everyday sense of 'existence', that is in the same sense as in, for instance, Mendeleyev's conjecture that 'there is' an element which he called 'eka-silicon' (now called 'germanium').

Michael Dummett has woven a subtle interpretation of the term 'realism', an interpretation which is probably quite different from the one I am using (see for instance Dummett (1982)). I am not, however, setting myself in opposition to Dummett. I am simply choosing not to set sail on those uncharted waters myself. I just claim that universals exist in the same sense as police and power poles—*whatever* sense that is. Another time, I might join Dummett in exploring what existence claims really mean, but not in this book.

In developing my Pythagorean philosophy of mathematics, I steer clear of epistemological issues as much as I can. I have some sympathy with Quine's epistemology for mathematics, and with Steiner's (1975, 1978) efforts at making a Quinean position compatible with some sort of broadly causal theory of knowledge: hoping by this manoeuvre to meet the challenging dilemma posed by Benacerraf in 'Mathematical Truth' (1973). But I also have some sympathy with attempts to give mathematics a more immediate foundation, if not in 'intuition' then at least in the *perception of patterns*: notable suggestions along these lines come from Maddy (1980) and Resnik (1975, 1981).

However, the most plausible epistemology I have yet seen for mathematics is that sketched by Kitcher in his recent book, *The Nature of Mathematical Knowledge* (1983). Kitcher urges a novel, historical perspective on the epistemology of mathematics. Each generation of mathematicians inherits a body of knowledge, and then adds to it. Most of what they know, they count as knowing simply because their teachers knew it; and most of what those teachers knew, they in turn counted as knowing simply because *their* teachers knew it; and so on, recursively, back into the mists of time.

This perspective, we may note, does not rule out all Quinean, causal, or perceptual sources for knowledge. At each stage in the process of growth, an increment is added to the knowledge we inherit from our teachers. Kitcher needs an independent, non-historical account of what makes these increments count as knowledge. For recent increments, a Quinean story sounds very plausible; for the earliest ones, a causal or perceptual story may apply.

Yet epistemology is not my concern in this book. I address the question of what numbers *are*, and not how we *know* about them.

I argue that numbers are universals. This theory obviously requires that some account be given of the nature of universals. I give a general characterization of what I mean by 'universals' in Part I, before going on to apply them to mathematics in Part II. The universals we study in mathematics, I claim, should be conceived as *recurrences*: their distinguishing feature is simply that they play fast and loose with space and time; many of them, for instance, can be found in two places at once.

Given the conception of universals outlined in Part I, I proceed in Part II to try to identify which universals the numbers are. In focusing on numbers, I take it that I will be covering the core of mathematics. This century, mathematics has expanded well beyond the study of numbers. It can no longer be entirely encapsulated in the definition which was standard from before Newton until the end of the last century: that mathematics is the study of *magnitude or quantity in general*. Nevertheless, number remains at the core of mathematics. And, indeed, number is probably the hardest part of mathematics to accommodate within the theory that mathematics is the study of universals. If numbers can be explained, then the rest of mathematics can be explained too.

In offering a theory of numbers, I undertake to give an interpretation of all the central kinds of numbers: natural numbers, integers, rational numbers, real numbers, and imaginary numbers. I begin with natural numbers. I construe each natural number n as an n-place relation. This account is not far removed from that described by Russell, in strikingly structuralist terms, in his *Introduction to Mathematical Philosophy* (1919, pp. 11–12):

A particular number is not identical with any collection of terms having that number: the number 3 is not identical with the trio consisting of Brown, Jones, and Robinson. The number 3 is something which all trios have in common, and which distinguishes them from other collections.

But though close to Russell's theory, mine is not quite the same as his. For Russell, 3 is a *property* of the collection, or set, containing Brown, Jones, and Robinson: for me it is a *relation among* Brown, Jones, and Robinson. *They are* three: the number three is not instantiated by any one thing, but rather, by any three distinct things.

I then move on to other sorts of numbers: the integers ('signed' numbers—positive and negative numbers); rational numbers (fractions); real numbers (infinite decimals); imaginary numbers (multiples of the square root of minus one); and complex numbers (combinations of all of the above). I treat all these kinds of numbers as fundamentally the same as one another, but fundamentally different from the natural numbers. Natural numbers are, I urge, universals which are instantiated directly by individuals in the world; but the other kinds of numbers cannot be construed as properties or relations of individuals, but rather, must be construed as *relations between relations*, using a technique pioneered by Frege (1893–1903) and Whitehead and Russell (1910–13).

I am grateful to a notorious pie-eater, Charles Pigden, for worrying me about whether natural numbers were really so very different from the rest: whether, as he insisted, he could eat three meat pies, or three-quarters of a meat pie, or root two meat pies, or pi meat pies, all in the same sense. But in the end I decided that the natural numbers can be construed at a deeper level than the rational or real or imaginary numbers ever could be. So I felt compelled to acknowledge a gulf between the natural numbers and the rest. On reflection (I claim) there is a greater difference between one pie and three-quarters of a pie, than between one pie and three pies. This can be highlighted by asking whether we are to estimate three-quarters of a pie by weight or by volume. And in Part II, I further illustrate the gulf between natural numbers and the rest, by exploring the ancient Pythagorean discovery that natural numbers are not the measure of all things, and that (as we would put it) real numbers are fundamentally different from natural numbers.

And besides, even if you could eat pi meat pies in the same sense that you can eat three meat pies, you surely cannot eat i, or $(a + ib)$ meat pies. Imaginary and complex numbers, at least, have to be treated as fundamentally different from natural numbers, even if real numbers do not. We need a dividing line somewhere. And by drawing a line between natural and real numbers, I make it possible to assimilate imaginary numbers to the reals. One of the things which pleased me most in the writing of this book was the neat way in which the Frege–Whitehead theory of real numbers can be extended to make sense of imaginary numbers. Imaginary numbers have long stood as a paradigm case of a mathematical notion which seems to refer to nothing real (and yet, miraculously, nevertheless to be useful). It is something of a triumph for a realist theory of mathematics to construe imaginary numbers as real *relations between relations*, with all the other sorts of numbers (except the natural numbers) falling out as simply special cases.

Understanding numbers has been my primary goal. But to understand mathematics today, it is also essential to get a clear picture of the nature and importance of *set theory*. I argue that set theory can be assimilated within my sort of Pythagorean perspective, by construing sets as universals of a special sort, akin to the universals with which I identify the natural numbers. I construe a set as a specific sort of relation holding among its members.

But whether or not I am right in my identification of sets with universals, my fundamental claim is that the reason why sets are so important in mathematics is that all the structures which mathematicians have hitherto wanted to study are *instantiated* by sets. Numbers are not really sets, despite what the textbooks say. The sets which the texts tell us the numbers *are*, are really just especially convenient examples of things which instantiate the numbers.

The motive for the excessive importance attributed to sets this century has been, in large measure, a desire to keep pure mathematics pure—a priori and entirely uninfected with the kind of uncertainty which is endemic in scientific method in general. In thus attempting to tailor our understanding of mathematics to meet epistemological preconceptions, I believe that such theories are putting the epistemological cart before the metaphysical horse. Knowledge is an attribute of persons; and persons are physical parts of a physical world. Thus we cannot hope to understand how people come to know things, prior to understanding the nature of the world in which they exist.

Nevertheless, the conception of pure mathematics as a priori has deep roots, and needs to be thoroughly excavated. In Part III, I try to hunt down the supposedly a priori source of sets and hence mathematics. The core idea is that of some way of inferring the *existence* of certain things from the *truth* of certain claims: a way of calling things into existence by linguistic magic—*defining* things into existence. I call the guiding idea behind this sort of linguistic magic the Truthmaker principle: when something is true then there must exist certain things which constitute its 'truthmaker'.

I allow that there may indeed be a route from truths to the existence of truthmakers of some sort or other. Yet, I argue, whatever these truthmakers are, they are *not* the subject-matter of mathematics. Thus, I refuse to set off down the only currently available road which promises to furnish mathematics with an a priori foundation. This sets mathematics on a footing comparable with that of the rest of the sciences. And that, I urge, is something we must learn to live with. Numbers are physical. So pure mathematics differs from the other sciences more in degree than in kind.

I METAPHYSICS

1 Mathematics and Universals

MATHEMATICIANS don't know what they are talking about. Who does? You may well ask. Yet in the case of mathematics, the problem of understanding what it's all about seems somehow even more acute than in the case of other subjects.

I ask myself, 'What are numbers?' I really want to know. So I search in mathematics textbooks for an answer. In book after book, I find that the few passages addressed to the problems which worry me most are very brief, often only five or six sentences, and are vague, metaphorical, and altogether unsatisfactory—in marked contrast to the clarity and precision of the mathematics which follows.

Consider for example Euclid's *Elements*. It begins with statements like 'A point is that which has no part. A line is breadthless length. The extremities of a line are points. A straight line is a line which lies evenly with the points on itself.' And yet, if you push on beyond these puzzling beginnings, the geometry which follows is breathtakingly wonderful. For all its much-vaunted rigour, contemporary mathematics is still very much like that.

I can bully myself into persisting with the study of mathematics, even in the absence of answers to my initial, philosophical questions. I don't know *what* numbers are, or *why* a minus times a minus makes a plus, or *how* we know that a square can be divided into two equal triangles, and so on; and yet nevertheless I can learn to get the right answers to many of the questions mathematicians ask. That is what mathematicians all have to do, if they are to get on with producing any new mathematics.

But *why* were my philosophical questions never answered? The reason is, I fear, simply that they are very hard to answer, and no one really knows the answers yet.

This whole book is devoted to the exploration of precisely those issues to which mathematics textbooks generally devote at most a sprinkling of sentences. I urge that our understanding of mathematics could be enhanced by rooting it more firmly in one of the central branches of metaphysics: the study of universals. Universals are the properties, relations, patterns, structures, and so forth, which can be shared in common by many diverse individual, particular things. Mathematics is often said to be 'abstract'. This is because it deals, not with particular things, but with properties which can be shared by many particular things. The problem of universals is the problem of understanding the nature of 'abstractions', and their relationship to particular, concrete things.

Metaphysics may thus be able to offer some help, not to mathematics itself, but rather, to our understanding of mathematics. I say this even though I am only too well aware that metaphysics is itself in a pretty sorry state, and badly in need of help—not just at its fringes, or deep down at its foundations, but through and through. Metaphysics runs a grave risk of degenerating into empty scholastic- ism if we approach it, again and again, by discussing the ancient texts in which the territory was first mapped out. And yet if each generation approaches the same old problems afresh, without an adequate historical sense, then all the same old doctrines will just be recycled over and over, in ever-changing rhetorical garb. This is why metaphysics sometimes seems to have made depressingly little progress over the last two millenniums—at least, it seems so if one reads only those discussions which are self-consciously directed toward the traditional problem of universals.

It is, perhaps, unwise to assume uncritically that *progress* is the only thing we should care about. Perhaps, sometimes, it may be worth transmitting cultural items relatively unchanged, indefinitely, like a beautiful heirloom. But the problem of universals is not a beautiful *theory* worth preserving—it is a *problem*, or a network of problems. A lack of progress in finding solutions is a legitimate object of concern.

The image one gets of metaphysics becomes more progressive, however, when viewed from a broader perspective, without restrict- ing ourselves to works which present themselves as being purely or primarily on a metaphysical issue like the problem of universals. Thus for instance much progress has been made in the understanding of the nature of biological species, especially since Darwin and Mendel. And the problem of species is within the ambit of the traditional problem of universals. The nature of species is still deeply problematic; but it is a progressive field of research in a way in which pure metaphysics often isn't.

And one's image of metaphysics changes still more radically if one begins to think of *mathematics* as *the theory of universals*. Mathematics has been spectacularly progressive over the last two millenniums. Of course, mathematics is laden with mysteries yet to be unravelled. And some of the mysteries at the foundational philosophical level have changed less than some of the more specialized branches of mathematics. And so at the basis of mathematics, in the explanation of the basic terms and axioms, the problems which still beset us are closely reminiscent of traditional metaphysical problems like the problem of universals. But even here, at the level where there has been the least transformation of ancient puzzles, even here progress has been and is being made. Traditional metaphysics can profit from cross-fertilization with its modern incarnation at the ground level of the vast edifice of contemporary mathematics. It is for this reason that my thinking about universals has been guided by the slogan: *Mathematics is the theory of universals*.

When I say mathematics *is* the theory of universals, I invite the objection:

Surely you must mean it is *part* of the theory of universals—you surely can't mean that *all* of the theory of universals is included within, or coextensive with mathematics. That would require us to assume that all properties and relations admit of mathematical treatment, and that furthermore everything interesting to say about them is said within mathematics. And that is surely too much to swallow.

I do take very seriously the equation between mathematics and the theory of universals. Yet perhaps, when pressed, I should retreat from claiming a strict identity between them. Perhaps some parts of the theory of universals fall outside mathematics. I have already mentioned the problems concerning biological species. And, in considering the intuitive oddity of subsuming the theory of universals under mathematics, it may be worth dwelling a little on the way in which *colours* figure so very prominently in traditional discussions, at least in the illustrations philosophers habitually draw upon during their investigations. If one wishes to mention a paradigm example of a *property* of objects, which property springs first to mind? Redness, I'll bet, or at any rate, colour. And yet colour is not part of the immediate subject-matter of mathematics. So how can I say the theory of universals is mathematics?

And yet the status of colour is very problematic. When probed closely, it is apt to evaporate into clouds of subjectivity. It is widely argued that, although material objects do appear to have various colours, they do not in fact have any such properties at all. Colour is only a property of our visual experience, and not of the objects which cause such experience. The relevant properties of the objects themselves are congeries of material properties such as the number and spatial relations of their atomic constituents—which in turn have properties like mass, velocity, and electric charge, but not colour—and which interact in various ways with different wavelengths of electromagnetic radiation.

At least since the time of Galileo it has been common to divide the apparent properties of material objects into two distinct categories, often called the *primary* and the *secondary* qualities. Colour is a secondary quality. Its status is problematic (in ways which stand over and above the ways in which the status of *any* property is problematic for the theory of universals). The primary qualities were listed by Locke as: solidity, extension, figure, motion or rest, and number (*An Essay Concerning Human Understanding*, Bk. II, S. VIII; see Cranston, 1965). It has not escaped attention that the qualities on Locke's list of primary qualities all admit of quantitative, mathematical treatment, except perhaps for solidity. Notice 'number', to start with: this being the subject-matter for arithmetic. 'Extension' and 'figure' are the subject-matter for geometry. And the theory of 'motion or rest' is what prompted Newton and Leibniz to develop the differential and integral calculus. Current physics might encourage some revisions to Locke's list of primary qualities; but such revisions would serve rather to reinforce than to undermine the striking overlap between primary qualities and the subject-matter of mathematics.

Thus, the subject-matter of mathematics does seem to extend at least over all the primary qualities of material objects. It is less clear whether it extends to any secondary qualities. This is no grave restriction if you take the view that things never really have, but only appear to have, such secondary qualities as colour. Yet if, on the other hand, you believe material objects do really have secondary qualities, then it is arguable that these secondary qualities must be identical with more or less complex combinations of primary qualities. *Warmth*, for instance, is listed as a secondary quality, and it is arguable that warmth is nothing over and above the average kinetic energy of the molecules in a body. If secondary qualities are really possessed by objects, then they are really just combinations of the primary qualities which constitute the subject-matter of mathematics. And so, it would seem, mathematics may embrace all actually instantiated universals, after all.

Some would argue, however, that secondary qualities, like colour, are instantiated by mental items, like visual experiences or visual images. This would seem to entail that mathematics treats only of those universals which are instantiated in the physical world, and not those which 'have their habitation only in the sensorium', as Galileo says in *The Assayer* (see Drake and O'Malley, 1960).

And yet it has also been argued that visual experiences are just physiological processes of some sort, within the human body. And, if these experiences *do* have secondary qualities like colour, perhaps their having a property like colour just amounts to their having some complex of neurological properties. And so, if secondary qualities are really possessed by experiential states, then they are arguably just combinations of the primary qualities which constitute the subject-matter of mathematics. And so, mathematics may embrace all instantiated universals after all, even if some of those universals should be experiential qualities of mental states. We can thus smuggle secondary qualities under the mathematical net, provided we are willing to accept some sort of a broadly physicalist account of the nature of experience. (See Borst (1970) for some recent classic debates over this issue.)

More cautiously put, the point is this. Secondary qualities initially seem to provide a knock-down objection to a strict identification between mathematics and the theory of universals. Yet on further reflection it becomes much less clear whether they constitute such a threat after all. And this applies to the problem of biological species as much as it does to colours.

The distinction between primary and secondary qualities has a long history. It was foreshadowed by Democritus in Fragment 9 (see for instance Kirk and Raven (1957, p. 422). In the seventeenth century, Galileo drew the distinction, very readably, in *The Assayer* (see Drake and O'Malley, 1960) and Descartes drew it in *The Principles of Philosophy*, Pt. IV, ss. 188–203 (see Haldane and Ross, 1970). The term 'secondary qualities' was coined by Robert Boyle, for instance in *The Origin of Forms and Qualities*, in the section called 'An Excursion about the Relative Nature of Physical Qualities' (see Birch, 1772). Newton also drew such a distinction in his *Opticks* (1730, Bk. I, Pt. 2).

The distinction between primary and secondary qualities has not, however, been without its critics, a notable early critic being Berkeley, for instance in his *Principles of Human Knowledge* (ss. 9–15), or in the first of his *Three Dialogues between Hylas and Philonous* (see Armstrong, 1965). The nature of the so-called secondary qualities remains contentious to this day.

And so, will I need to weaken my slogan: 'Mathematics is the theory of universals'? Perhaps I will some day; but not until several disputed doctrines concerning secondary qualities have been firmly settled in the negative. Until then, if asked to choose between Galileo and Berkeley, I choose Galileo. And if forced to ascribe secondary qualities to experiences, I will fall back on some sort of physicalist theory of experiences, which rests such experiential qualities on the primary qualities of neurological states of the organism.

Suppose then that all actually instantiated universals were agreed to fall within the subject-matter of mathematics. Even so, one might argue that mathematics studies only some, and not all, of the interesting things which may be *said about* those universals. So the scope of the theory of universals may be taken to be broader than the scope of mathematics. Perhaps mathematics only discusses a small range of unusually neat and tidy interrelationships among universals.

There are indeed many interesting facts about universals which fall outside what we think of as mathematics. There are, for instance, facts about *which* things have *which* properties and relations. Some such facts may perhaps fall under pure mathematics (the fact that 4 is even, say); many more such facts may fall under applied mathematics. Yet not all such facts would be counted as part of mathematics, even broadly construed. Some may count as physics; others as geography or history; others as everyday common knowledge. A fact, for instance, concerning the mass of my baggage at an airport customs desk will be of interest only briefly, and to very few people.

There are facts about universals which are not part of the theory of universals. A theory about a given subject-matter is a systematic collection of statements about the relations among the things falling within that subject-matter. So the theory of universals will be a systematic collection of statements about the relations among universals. And that, I claim, is precisely what mathematics is. Pure mathematics is maximally unconcerned with the relations of universals to concrete individuals. As the proportion of concern given to concrete individuals rises, pure mathematics shades off, through applied mathematics, into other subjects.

And so I return again to the contention that mathematics is the theory of universals. In mathematics, we study *the relations among relations*.

I hope this perspective will help us to understand mathematics better. But I also intend it to have methodological repercussions for metaphysics. We should tailor our metaphysics to fit existing mathematics as comfortably as possible.

2   Recurrence

SOME schools of ancient Buddhists argued for something called a 'no self' doctrine, and more generally, for a principle of *impermanence*, a doctrine of *momentariness*. It was argued by some that nothing exists except 'point-instants'. These Buddhist theories are reminiscent of various things in the Western tradition, notably the Heraclitean doctrine of universal flux, and David Hume's *Treatise of Human Nature*, Bk. I, s. 6, 'Of personal identity' (see Selby-Bigge, 1960). But the Buddhists seem to have pursued doctrines of momentariness with a remarkable degree of single-mindedness. See for instance *Buddhist Logic* (Stcherbatsky, 1962), Appendix V on Buddhist nominalism; and *Outlines of Indian Philosophy* (Hiriyana, 1932, Chs. 5 and 9).

The Buddhists argued that nothing can exist at two distinct points of space at a given time. Before instruction you might think otherwise, you might point to two distinct places, and say for instance: 'Surely there is a chariot *here*, and that same chariot is *there* too.' But the Buddhist reply should be that what is *here* is one thing, a hub say, and what is *there* is something else, a spoke say. A hub and a spoke are two distinct things; so we do not, after all, have the same thing in both of these two places.

An analogous conclusion was drawn with regard to time: nothing can exist at two distinct moments of time. We may think for instance that a flame may last through the night; but this, it is argued, is an illusion. What exists in the morning may be very similar to what existed in the evening, but it is in fact a numerically distinct thing. It is composed of different matter, is no doubt of a slightly different shape, and probably in a different place (especially if we take into account the movement of the Earth). It is really a different, albeit similar, thing. And a person, too, is really just like a flame. The child and the adult are distinct things: there is no single thing which survives through adolescence. And, in general, there is no single thing which exists at two distinct moments of time.

This theory is powerful and appealing. Yet I will advance a philosophy of mathematics which requires us to free ourselves from the grip of this picture. We must free ourselves from the presumption that everything there is must be somewhere, and nowhere else. A number, for instance, is not to be found at just one point-instant, and nowhere else. If nothing existed, except what exists at just one point-instant, then numbers would not exist. And that is the sort of mathematical nihilism which I am setting out to oppose.

As a first step in loosening the grip of the Buddhist's picture, we may draw upon the notion of an *aggregate* of distinct point-instants. An aggregate of point-instants is to be regarded as a single thing which has each of those point-instants as parts. (See Goodman (1966), for a thorough exploration of the theory of aggregates.)

We may agree that what is *here* is a hub, and what is *there* is a spoke, and that a hub is not identical with a spoke; yet we may also say that a *chariot* is a thing which includes the hub as one part and the spoke as another. Since one part of the chariot is here, and the other is there, we may legitimately say that the chariot is the sort of thing which can occupy two distinct places at once. The chariot is both here, where the hub is, and there, where the spoke is.

Similar comments apply in the case of time. We may take a flame to be an aggregate of point-instants, each one distinct from the others, but each a part of one and the same temporally extended aggregate which we call a single flame.

The flame can be pictured as an aggregate of aggregates: it is an aggregate, a succession, of things we may call *time-slices*. Each time-slice, in turn, is an aggregate of point-instants which are simultaneous with one another. Thus construed, a flame may be said to exist at different moments of time, by virtue of containing one time-slice existing at one of those times, and another time-slice existing at the other of those times.

This is sometimes called the 'four-dimensionalist' account of enduring objects, since it treats existence at different moments of time in much the same way that most people treat the existence of things like chariots across different locations in the three dimensions of space. Just as an extended object, say a loaf of sliced bread, has different parts in each of the places it occupies, so too an enduring object has different parts, time-slices, which succeed one another through time, and constitute a single aggregate which contains each time-slice as a part.

Modern physics forces us to be careful in wielding the image of time-slices. Einstein has taught us that two distinct point-instants may count as simultaneous relative to one frame of reference, and not simultaneous relative to another. So, from another frame of reference, they would belong to two distinct time-slices. An object should thus be thought of, primarily, as an aggregate directly of point-instants, like an unsliced loaf which will be carved into time-slices in different ways, from different frames of reference. What exist are point-instants, or space-time points; the ordering of these into a temporal sequence is relative, not absolute. But the relativity of the division into slices does not undermine the overall four-dimensionalist account of enduring objects, as aggregates of parts, each of which exists at a single space-time point.

By construing some things as aggregates of others, we relax the Buddhist picture a little; but not enough to give breathing-space for the sort of realist interpretation I think mathematics needs. If nothing existed except aggregates of point-instants, then there would be no numbers. A number is not the sort of thing which has distinct parts at each of several space-time points. So the Buddhist picture needs to be loosened further.

The first loosening I will mention concerns the persistence of objects through time. There was once a school of Greek philosophers called *atomists*, who held that all that exists is a collection of many indestructible atoms, falling through the void, and rearranging themselves to form all the manifold phenomena we observe in nature. See for instance *The Presocratic Philosophers* (Kirk and Raven 1957, ch. 17).

The key feature distinguishing the atomists' picture from that of the Buddhists, is the part played by the persistence of the atoms. One and the same atom is conceived as existing at every distinct moment of time. And the atom exists at different moments in a different sense from that in which an aggregate of Buddhist point-instants may be said to exist at two different moments. The atom does not consist of distinct parts, each existing at distinct moments.

According to some conceptions, an atom is supposed to have no parts. But this may not be true of all conceptions of atoms; perhaps on some conceptions an atom may be said to *have* parts, and yet nevertheless be indivisible in the sense that it is impossible to spatially scatter those parts. We are nudged in that direction by reflecting on the fact that the atoms of the ancient Greeks were supposed to have a variety of *shapes*. This presumably meant that they could occupy more than a single point of space at a given time. It is easy to slip from this to the conclusion that they must contain distinct parts at those distinct points of space. Yet is is worth considering, also, the notion that perhaps atoms should be conceived as having no parts, even though they do have shape. On such a view, an atom could occupy more than one place at a given time, without having distinct parts at each of those places. It would occupy a *region* of space, without having distinct parts occupying each of the sub-regions of that region.

In fact, on reflection, one may become uncomfortable with the Buddhist picture of point-instants, because one may well become dubious about the very existence of any such things as points or instants. An interval of time is real enough, but an instant of time, a moment, something with no duration whatever, may well seem a mere abstraction. Similarly, a region of space is real enough, but a point of space, something with no size at all, may well seem a non-existent but merely imagined *limit* of a nested sequence of progressively smaller and smaller finite regions. On such a view, all that exist are regions of space-time, and there are no point-instants. Hence there can be nothing which does *not* occupy more than one location at any given time.

A theory which allows regions, but not points, may nevertheless require that anything occupying a region must contain distinct parts occupying each sub-region. The consequence of this theory is that everything is made up of distinct parts, its parts are made up of parts, and so on *ad infinitum*. This view is compatible with one conception of atomism—the conception on which an atom is 'indivisible' only in the sense that its parts cannot be separated from one another.

Nevertheless, the idea that everything is composed of parts does run against the spirit of atomism. It is in some ways more natural to construe atomism as claiming that atoms are indivisible because they *do not have* parts. Combine this with the idea that atoms do have shape; and the result is a doctrine according to which it is possible for a thing to occupy a region of space, to be located at various different point-instants, even though it does *not* have distinct parts at each of those point-instants.

This loosens our thinking significantly. It allows that the same thing can be present at different times, and in two different places at the same time, without being an aggregate of distinct parts. This view can be abbreviated by saying: 'The same thing can be wholly present at different times or at different places at the same time.' The phrase 'wholly present' implies that it is not just a part of the thing which is present at each different place; it does *not* mean that it is present at that place *and no other*. When something occupies a region, in the way in which a partless atom would occupy a region, then that thing is, in the required sense, wholly present at each point in the region.

Yet now our conception of an atom has lurched perilously close to the traditional conception of a *universal*. A universal—a property for instance—is the sort of thing which can be wholly present at different locations at the same time. The only difference between universals, thus characterized, and partless, shaped atoms, would seem to be that the locations occupied by an atom form a spatio-temporally con-tinuous, connected region. Universals are permitted to occupy scattered regions; the same property may be present in each of two widely separated, disconnected regions. And a property may have intermittent existence, in a way that is not normally permitted for atoms: there may be times when a property exists nowhere, between times when it exists in various regions. For an atom, the existence of the atom in a particular place at one given time is tightly connected, causally, with its presence in other places, at various later times. In contrast, the presence of a property at one place at one time is only loosely connected with its presence at another place at another time.

The whole notion of the *location* of universals is, in fact, highly problematic. A property of located things is usually thought of as located wherever the things are that have that property. But if the thing that has that property is extended through a region of space (either as an aggregate, or not), then it may not be possible to locate the property anywhere in particular within that region. It may be tempting, for instance, to locate the *mass* of an object at its *centre of gravity*, but this choice of location must not be pressed too hard. And for many other properties, there is not even a prima-facie location to give them within the region occupied by an object. Where for instance is my height, or my age? Or consider the problem of locating an object's shape. The best we can do is to say that such properties exist within the region occupied by the object, but they do not have distinct parts at each point within that region.

Properties of located objects can thus be located, after a fashion. But *relations* are somewhat more problematic, even when they are instantiated by clearly locatable objects. Consider a relationship holding between two individuals which are some distance apart: two sisters perhaps. *Where* is the relationship between them?

One could perhaps say that a relationship between two individuals is not located anywhere. Yet one is not compelled to take that stand. We could say, rather, that a relationship between two individuals is located within any region which contains both those individuals. But it is not possible to locate a relationship any more precisely than that.

When a universal is instantiated by located individuals, then such a universal can, in some sense, be located within regions of space. Of course, we must allow that several different universals may be within the same region at the same time; and that the same universal may be within several different, disconnected regions at the same time. This promiscuousness of a universal's relations to regions of space is enough to set many moralistic philosophers against relations altogether. They seek, at all costs, to avoid admitting that any such things exist at all. And yet such opposition to relations, based solely on their spatial promiscuity, rests on sheer prejudice. This prejudice should be resisted, especially if we wish to make sense of mathematics.

Indeed, the whole notion of *locating* things should be regarded with deep suspicion, even in cases where it has generally been thought to be unproblematic. Relationships are, in general, contingent, and cannot be legislated a priori. Even if certain relationships are necessary, we should be wary of legislating from a priori. And this applies to the relationships between things and regions of space as much as it does to other sorts of relationships. We have no license to make strong a priori assumptions about how things *must* be related to regions of space. Why should we assume that two things can never be in the same place at the same time? Why should we assume that a single thing can never be in two different places at the same time? We should not assume these things; we may conjecture that these things are so, and indeed they may be so. But then again, they may not.

My suspicions about locality have been vastly deepened by dabbling in books about quantum mechanics. A great deal of idealist fog has clouded discussions of quantum mechanics, and I do not find idealism the least bit tempting. But among attempts to interpret quantum mechanics *realistically*, that is to say, as a literally true description of an objective, non-mental reality, the only attempts which show any promise are ones which loosen up our assumptions about the *locations* of the small constituents of material objects.

An electron, for instance, is normally thought of as a particular, an individual—and not a universal. And yet it is quite unclear whether an electron does have any location at all during periods when it is not interacting, or exchanging energy, with anything else (or, as it is very misleadingly put, when it is not being 'observed').

In a famous paper, 'Can Quantum-Mechanical Description of Physical Reality be Considered Complete?', Einstein, Podolsky, and

Rosen (1935) argued that quantum mechanics cannot be interpreted as providing a complete description of an objective reality. One of the key premisses they used, however, one of the key assumptions which makes it so very hard to interpret quantum mechanics realistically, is an assumption sometimes known as *separability*. Suppose, for instance, that two electrons undergo certain sorts of interactions under a special experimental arrangement, and then part of the apparatus is flown to Athens, and part is shipped to Bombay. The assumption of separability would then tell us that we cannot say that both of the electrons are located in Athens *and* that both of the electrons are located in Bombay. Someone in Athens could not look at the apparatus there, and say: 'There is an electron here which is also located in Bombay; indeed, there are two such electrons here.'

Separability is a very natural assumption to make—as natural as atomism. Yet the Einstein–Podolsky–Rosen argument should make us less comfortable in making such an assumption, however natural it may feel. Their argument has been reinforced recently by what is known as Bell's Inequality (see for instance Bell (1964, 1966)). It is still not altogether clear what conclusions should be drawn from these observations on the nature of quantum mechanics, except that very little can be taken for granted. Perhaps we should conclude, with Einstein, that quantum mechanics fails to describe fully and consistently the nature of objective physical reality. Or perhaps we should conclude that there is no objective reality. Or perhaps we should conclude, rather, that we should radically rethink our assumptions about locality. I hope the truth lies along the last of these paths.

Some of Dirac's philosophical comments, in the third edition of his *Principles of Quantum Mechanics*, strike me as very deep, and as opening the way towards a promising realist interpretation of quantum mechanics (Dirac, 1947). The now more or less orthodox, so-called Copenhagen interpretation, may perhaps be seen as embodying the core of Dirac's realist interpretation, under a heavy sludge of unappealing positivist and idealist ideology. What is so very admirable about Dirac is that, although some positivist inclinations are visible, nevertheless, they are carefully restrained and do not unduly distort the picture he presents.

The intriguing idea which Dirac brings to light is that, surprising as it may seem, there *could* be an electron which is located both in Athens and in Bombay. Or perhaps one should say there could be an electron which is not located anywhere, but which has a certain probability of coming to exist in Athens, and a certain probability of coming to exist in Bombay. Or perhaps we might try a third alternative: that there is some *degree* to which it is present in Athens, and a *degree* to which it is present in Bombay. The probability that it will come to exist wholly in Athens will then depend on the degree to which it is there already.

On this last conception, location is not an all-or-nothing matter. The relation of an electron to a region of space may be the sort of relationship which admits of degrees—anything from a faint flirtation to wholesale imprisonment.

Dirac makes it clear that if such an attitude is taken towards the location of an individual, then the same attitude should be taken to various of its other qualities as well. A photon of light for instance, Dirac suggests, should not be thought of as always having just a single plane of polarization; rather, either we should say it has no single plane of polarization, or we should say it has various different polarizations to various different degrees.

This makes the relationship between 'individuals' and 'universals' rather more complex than we have generally assumed. We have assumed that either an individual 'has' a property, or it does not. I suggest that the relationship between an individual and a property may admit of degrees. This is not to say that an individual can both have and not have a property. Nor is it to say there is no truth of the matter concerning the relationship of the individual to the property. Rather, it is to say that there *is* a determinate truth about the *degree* to which an individual has any given property.

And yet, this way of talking is somewhat misleading. The very terms 'individual' and 'property' need to be regarded with suspicion. In rethinking our deepest assumptions about locality, we may be subverting the whole traditional distinction between particulars and universals. The failure of locality of an electron makes the electron, in some ways, rather closer to the traditional conception of a universal. Perhaps one could redescribe the case of a bi-located electron, by saying that there is a region of Athens which is 'this-electron-ish', and a region of Bombay which is also 'this-electron-ish', at the same time. The property of 'this-electron-hood' can be present in two disconnected regions at the same time, because it is a universal. Or so we might say.

However, the best attitude to take is simply one of extreme suspicion about all assumptions concerning locality. Among the things there are, it may or may not be possible to draw a sharp line between spatially restrained 'particulars', and spatially promiscuous 'universals'. Some things may turn out to be multiply located, and some of these may perhaps be appropriately described as universals, for that reason. It is tempting to call them *abstract*, too, but I am unhappy with that term because of the metaphysical baggage it carries with it. The term 'abstract' suggests that the things it applies to are causally impotent—that they have no causes or effects; and it implies that they are generated by some sort of process of 'abstraction' which creates entities that exist only as 'objects of thought'. I am not advocating the existence of 'abstract' objects in *that* sense. What I urge is only more open-mindedness about where one should look for the things there are.

The question, 'Where is it?' is thus much less straightforward than you might have thought. It is important to recognize this when thinking about the interpretation of mathematics. Some of the first worries which strike people in the philosophy of mathematics concern the fact that mathematical entities like numbers cannot be located anywhere in particular in space.

Numerals, like the word 'four', and the symbol '4', and so forth, all exist—it may be said—since you can see and locate them; but there is *nowhere* that you can find something which is *referred* to by one of these numerals. This leads many to doubt whether numerals refer to anything at all. And this generates the illusion that mathematics is concerned only with the manipulation of meaningless, or at any rate referenceless, symbols.

Yet this whole drift of thought is deeply misconceived. It is not, after all, so very clear just where a numeral should be located. If I write a numeral twice—2 . . . 2—then doesn't the same numeral occur in two different places at the same time? Numerals, on one natural construal, are *types* of sound or inscription, rather than individual marks or sounds. They are of a kind with universals, rather than particulars, and especially tricky universals at that. Shape may be relevant to determining that '2' and '2' are tokens of the same numeral; but the more you look into the matter, the more complex it becomes. Some variation of shape is clearly permissible, as for instance between different typefaces. Or between type and handwriting . . . or indeed between written and spoken language. And in some typefaces, the only difference between '6' and '9' lies in the relative orientation of other, nearby tokens. Numerals are not only universals;

they are in fact more of a piece with secondary qualities than with primary qualities. It is largely their relationships to human agents that make different tokens count as tokens of the same numeral.

Someone with a hang-up about locality might draw the conclusion that numbers are nothing over and above *tokens* of numerals, nothing over and above individual marks and noises. And yet this interpretation begins to lose much of the intuitive plausibility initially possessed by the suggestion that numbers are 'just symbols'.

The impetus towards identifying numbers with symbols derives largely from Buddhist or atomist assumptions about locality. Once we have cast off those assumptions, the impossibility of locating numbers in any (single) region of space can no longer be used as a good reason for denying their existence. The tenuousness of their relationship to space and time presses us, rather, to think of numbers as *universals*, as traditionally conceived.

However, the traditional conception of universals has two tap-roots. One of these is better fitted than the other to nourish our understanding of mathematics. The first of these tap-roots lies in the recognition of *recurrence*. It is this fact of recurrence that I have been tracing, in exploring the notion of locality; and it is the resulting conception of universals which can nourish a healthy, realist interpretation of mathematics.

The second tap-root for theories of universals is quite different, and makes the link between mathematics and metaphysics much more problematic. It will wait in the wings until Part III. Until then, I ask you to think of universals as things just like individuals, except for the fact that they are more promiscuous in their relationships with regions of space-time. Mathematical objects, like numbers, are things of that sort. They have nothing distinctive to do with predication and they cannot be magically called into existence by a mere definition.

o : x :: x : o

II MATHEMATICS

3 Pebbles and Pythagoras

It is a striking fact about natural numbers that there are no two
natural numbers n and m such that

$$n^2 = 2m^2.$$

(By the natural numbers I mean . . . 3, 2, 1 but not 0.) If there were
two such numbers n and m then by simple algebraic transformations,
we could derive

$$\sqrt{2} = n/m.$$

That is, the square root of 2 would then be a rational number—a
fraction. But there is no fraction which is the square root of 2. And so,
you may infer, the square root of 2 is not a fraction. But beware! There
is a world of difference between saying that there is no fraction which
is the square root of 2, and saying that the square root of 2 is not a
fraction. This will become clear in what follows.

There are many ways of proving that there are no natural numbers
for which $n^2 = 2m^2$. The usual way is by supposing there were such
numbers, applying various algebraic transformations, and deducing a
contradiction. See for instance Heath (1921, p. 91).

Yet the usual proof uses algebraic notation which was not available
to the early Greeks. And in addition, it obscures the true nature of the
discovery. The irrationality of root 2 is made to seem a consequence of
certain algebraic rules for manipulating symbols. That is not what it
is, nor is it how it would have appeared to the early Greeks.

By the time of Plato, Aristotle, and Euclid, mathematics had been
firmly cast into a geometrical mould. So the proof of the irrationality
of root 2 was presented as a geometrical fact. And indeed, the *existence*
of something which can be called root 2 does emerge very strikingly in
geometry (though it can be found in non-geometrical contexts as
well).

Yet it is a purely arithmetical fact that *there are no* natural numbers
for which $n^2 = 2m^2$. Such a purely arithmetical fact should have a
purely arithmetical demonstration.

I will display the arithmetical fact, that necessarily $n^2 \neq 2m^2$, by using only techniques which the early Greeks are known to have used when they displayed numbers by arranging patterns of pebbles.

The pebble proof I offer will serve several purposes. For one thing, it will present a case-study to keep in mind when reflecting on the nature of mathematics. Too often, I find, philosophies of mathematics never ever mention any real mathematics; and this aggravates the risk that the philosophical reflections will lose touch with mathematical practice, and with mathematics itself. To be more specific, I hope that a look at a simple proof of the non-existence of a rational square root of 2 will help to underline the fundamental distinction which I claim separates natural from real numbers. I hope it will add to the plausibility of the theory I will offer concerning the natural numbers, and to the quite distinct theory I offer concerning the nature of real numbers. Natural numbers are instantiated by pebbles; real numbers are not.

Some heaps of pebbles can be rearranged in various ways, to yield various patterns—triangles, rectangles, and so forth. A heap of fifteen, for instance, can be arranged to make either a triangle or a rectangle (see Fig. 1).

```
        0
      0   0
    0   0   0                        0  0  0  0  0
  0   0   0   0          =           0  0  0  0  0
0   0   0   0   0                     0  0  0  0  0
```

FIG. 1

Some heaps of pebbles can be arranged in a square grid with as many rows as columns; and some such square grids can be rearranged to yield two smaller square grids (as in Fig. 2).

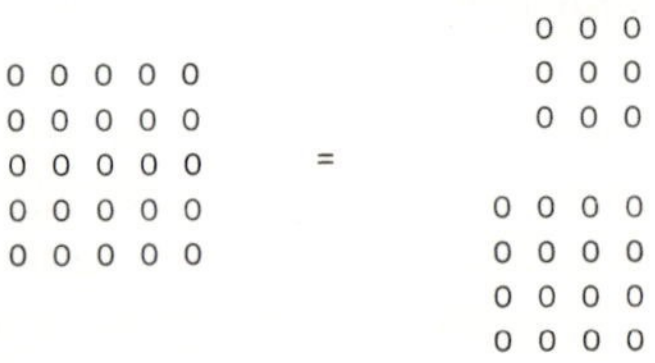

```
                                    0  0  0
        0 0 0 0 0                   0  0  0
        0 0 0 0 0                   0  0  0
        0 0 0 0 0      =
        0 0 0 0 0                0  0  0  0
        0 0 0 0 0                0  0  0  0
                                0  0  0  0
                                0  0  0  0
```

$$(5^2 = 4^2 + 3^2)$$

FIG. 2

Now I ask: *Can any square grid of pebbles ever be rearranged to make two EQUAL smaller squares?*

The answer is, No; since if there were any such square grid, then there would be natural numbers for which $n^2 = 2m^2$, and we know that there are no such natural numbers.

Yet it is a fact about pebbles that there is no such square array of pebbles. It even feels like a 'physical' fact about pebbles, and not a fact about whether specified transformation rules can lead from $n^2 = 2m^2$ to a contradiction. It should be possible to demonstrate it just by reflecting *on pebbles*, without any detour through algebraic manipulations of symbols.

Suppose there were a square array which could be rearranged to yield two equal smaller squares; and suppose this square, and its two clones, were the ones pictured in Fig. 3. We know in advance that the

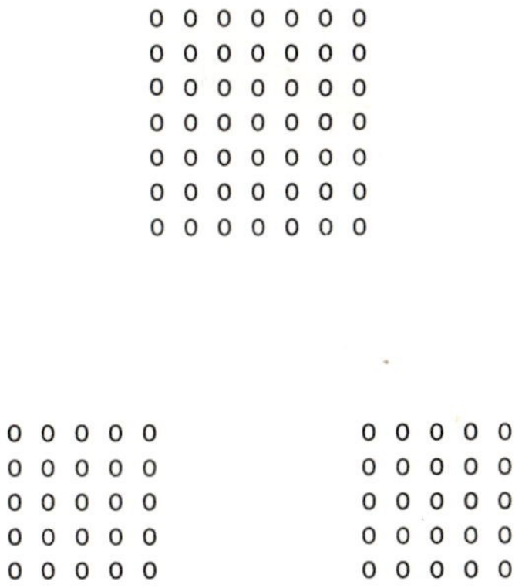

```
0 0 0 0 0 0 0
0 0 0 0 0 0 0
0 0 0 0 0 0 0
0 0 0 0 0 0 0
0 0 0 0 0 0 0
0 0 0 0 0 0 0
0 0 0 0 0 0 0
```

```
0 0 0 0 0            0 0 0 0 0
0 0 0 0 0            0 0 0 0 0
0 0 0 0 0            0 0 0 0 0
0 0 0 0 0            0 0 0 0 0
0 0 0 0 0            0 0 0 0 0
```

FIG. 3

larger square I have used for illustrative purposes *cannot* be equal to the two smaller ones. But count to make sure! The larger one contains $7^2 = 49$; the two smaller squares together contain $(5^2 + 5^2) = 50$. The larger square is *almost* equal to the two smaller ones. It is a surprising fact that, no matter how big the larger square is, it can never equal two smaller equal squares. Why can't it?

Theorem (Pebble Pythagoras)

Suppose there were some large square array A which equals two smaller equal squares B and C. For illustrative purposes, take A to be the 7×7 square above, and B and C to be the two 5×5 squares above.

Imagine setting out to rearrange A to yield B and C, in the following way. First, we simply carve B out of A, as in Fig. 4.

```
o o o o o o o
o o o o o o o
o o                    o o o o o
o o                    o o o o o
o o                    o o o o o
o o                    o o o o o
o o                    o o o o o

Remainder of A                 B
```

FIG. 4

The remainder of A then needs to be rearranged to make a square C equal to B. To do this, we must rearrange the pebbles in the two small 'tails', shown in Fig. 5, putting a pebble, o, on each of the unoccupied positions, x, in the square C that we are endeavouring to construct. But this entails that the square of x's would have to be equal to the two 'tails'.

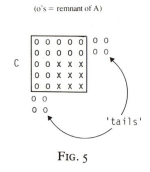

(o's = remnant of A)

```
      o o o o | o o
      o o o o | o o
C     o o x x x
      o o x x x
      o o x x x
      o o
      o o          'tails'
```

FIG. 5

Call the square of x's a, and the two 'tails' b and c.

The 'tails' b and c must be squares. The top 'tail' was formed by removing from A as many rows as there are in B, and then as many columns as there are in C. There are as many rows in B as columns in C; and there were as many rows as columns in the original square A. Equals taken from equals leave equals: so the top 'tail' has as many rows as columns. Similarly for the other 'tail'.

Hence, in order to rearrange the large square A to make two equal smaller squares B and C, we would have to rearrange another two equal smaller squares b and c to make a square a. For *every* square A which can be divided into two equal squares, there will be a smaller square a which can be divided into two equal squares.

It follows that *there is no smallest heap of pebbles*, and that is absurd. Or it follows that *if* we were to have a square array of pebbles which could be divided into two equal squares, *then* we could divide this square into smaller and smaller squares *ad infinitum* without ever running out of pebbles. And that is impossible.

The supposition that any square A equals two smaller squares B and C must therefore be false, since it entails absurd consequences.

We may sum this up in Fig. 6. If a ≠ b + c, then A ≠ B + C. If we know that a ≠ b + c for the smaller squares a, b and c, then it follows for the larger squares A, B, and C too, that A ≠ B + C. Any square A thus *inherits* a difference between itself and any two equal squares B and C; this difference is inherited from a difference between smaller squares from which A is constructed. This chain of inheritance traces right back to the difference between 3^2 and $(2^2 + 2^2)$; or, further, to the difference between 1^2 and $(1^2 + 1^2)$. And this is why no square A can equal two smaller squares B and C, which was to be shown.

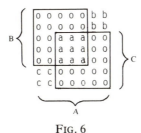

FIG. 6

And yet, if we turn to geometry, we find that any square *area* can *always* be divided into two smaller equal squares. Divide any square A into four triangles, by drawing in its diagonals; and then these four triangles can be arranged to make two equal squares, as shown in Fig. 7.

This, together with Pebble Pythagoras, shows that square areas cannot be finite sums of indivisible atomic parts, and that space is therefore infinitely divisible.

It also shows that there can be *no common measure* for the side of the large square A and the side of the small squares B or C. That is to say, there is no shorter length, however short, which could be chosen as

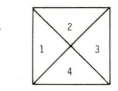

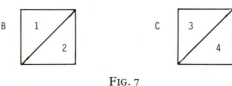

FIG. 7

a *unit* length, and which could divide the side of A exactly and the side of B exactly. If there were, then A could be divided into equal small squares, like graph paper; and so could B and C (see Fig. 8). A pebble could be placed on each of the small squares within A, B, and C, and we would have constructed a square grid A equal to two smaller square grids B and C, which is impossible.

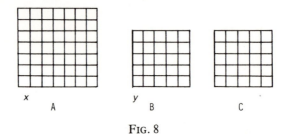

FIG. 8

The small squares in A cannot be equal in *number* to those in B and C together. And yet the area of A does equal the area of B and C together. So the area of the number of squares in A equals the area of a different number of squares in B and C. Hence the squares in A cannot all be equal in area to the squares in B and C. It follows that the length x, which evenly divides the side of A, cannot equal any length y which evenly divides the sides of B or C.

I will return to the incommensurability of lengths later. First, I want to dwell on the purely arithmetical fact that there can be no heap of pebbles which can be arranged as a single square grid, and then rearranged as two equal smaller square grids. This is a fact about pebbles; and it involves no geometrical notions at all: it makes no reference to lengths or areas or anything else geometrical.

What has been proved, then, is a fact about pebbles. What properties and relations enter into this proof? I claim that numbers are universals. The question is, *which* universals are the numbers? Let us search among the properties and relations employed in the pebble proof. If numbers are indeed universals, they must be among the properties and relations which appear in the proof of Pebble Pythagoras.

4 Numbers as Properties

ONE thing which keeps cropping up in Pebble Pythagoras is *modality*. The proof establishes something to be *impossible*. And the proof relies on claims about ways in which pebbles *could* be arranged and rearranged. It is argued, for instance, that *if* you could arrange a heap of pebbles in a certain way, then (necessarily) you could rearrange them in some other way. Conceptions of what is possible, impossible, necessary, and so forth, leap out at you from even the simplest of mathematical proofs. Modality is a huge mystery to me, and I would love to have a clearer understanding of it. One of my key motives for exploring metaphysics and mathematics has been the desire to get a clearer grip on modality. My hunch is that modal claims rest on facts about relations among universals. When we say that one pattern of pebbles *could* be rearranged to yield another, what we are really saying is that some relationship holds between these two patterns. Presumably, the relevant relationship will be something like that of 'containing as many pebbles as'. It is immaterial whether we ever compel any actual pebbles to instantiate those patterns. But let modality simmer in the background for now.

One of the key universals appearing in Pebble Pythagoras is a property of arrays of pebbles—the property of *being a square grid*. This involves the property of having as many rows as columns. This in turn involves the property of being a row or column of pebbles, which rests on the property of being a line of pebbles. Also crucial is the relation, *containing as many pebbles as*. Pick an aggregate which has the property of being a row of pebbles, and pick another which has the property of being a column of pebbles: and if we are dealing with a square grid, the first aggregate will *contain as many pebbles as* the second aggregate.

It is tempting to take numbers to be properties of aggregates—properties of heaps of pebbles, or herds of elephants, flocks of sheep, schools of fish, bevies of beauties, covens of witches, coveys of partridges, bands of men, swarms of bees, troops of kangaroos, packs of wolves, hosts of angels, stacks of books, bunches of grapes, and so forth. Such a theory has been held by the British empiricist philosopher, John Stuart Mill, for instance in his *System of Logic*, Bk. II, chs. 5 and 6 (see Robson, 1973). I have been strongly influenced by a recent defence of Mill, by D. M. Armstrong (1978, especially vol. II, ch. 18, s. V).

When you look closely at Pebble Pythagoras, you will see that *there are* properties of aggregates which figure importantly in the proof, and which seem at least to have a great deal to do with natural numbers. A theory which takes numbers to be properties of aggregates has considerable initial appeal.

And yet Mill's theory of numbers was vigorously attacked by Frege, in many places, but especially in his *Grundlagen*, pt. II, s. 23 (see Austin, 1968). Frege's arguments have convinced nearly everyone, and Armstrong is swimming against the tide in trying to revive Mill.

Nevertheless, let us look at Frege's arguments. One of his arguments can be dismissed fairly swiftly. Frege protests that things do not need to be physically *aggregated* (brought *close together*) in order to have a number. Yet this would only count against a version of Mill's theory, according to which an aggregate of things exists only when those things are close together. These days, since for instance *The Structure of Appearance* (Goodman, 1966), theories permitting the existence of scattered, or even spatially unrelated, aggregates have become very much a live possibility. On any such theory of aggregates, Frege's objection to Mill falls flat.

Frege's key argument—the one which has been most persuasive—has been this. Suppose an aggregate, like the array of pebbles A, could be said to have a number. Which number does it have? The obvious first answer is that, since it contains 49 pebbles, it must have the number-property 49. And yet it also contains 7 rows; so why should we not say it has the number-property 7? And God only knows how many molecules it contains. If the aggregate were to be conceived as having *any* number-properties, then it would have to have *many* different number-properties. And Frege thinks this is absurd. He thinks that one and the same thing cannot have both the number 49, and the number 7, . . . and so on. Hence number is not a property of aggregates.

Frege's own theory took off from the idea that number arises, not from properties of aggregates, but from properties of properties. It is not the aggregate A which has the property 49, but rather, it is the property of *being a pebble in A*, which has the number-property of having 49 instances. In contrast, the property of *being a row in A* has the different number-property of having only 7 instances.

Armstrong rightly resists Frege's argument. Frege assumes that if numbers were properties of aggregates, then the number-property 49 and the number-property 7 would be incompatible properties: that it would be impossible for the same thing to be both 49 and 7. Of course, the same thing could not *be identical with* both 49 and 7, but that does not show that it could not *have* both the property 49 and the property 7. Frege might be right, different number-properties might be incompatible, but this would have to be argued.

To undermine Frege's assumption, Armstrong asks us to consider properties of the sort: *having 49 parts*, and *having 7 parts*. One and the same thing can indeed have both of these properties. Armstrong then asks us to consider the conjecture that each number *n* can be identified with the property of *n-partedness*. If this conjecture were correct, if a number were just a property of being so-many-parted, then Frege's key anti-Mill argument would be blocked.

I agree with Armstrong that there are such properties as being 7-parted. So I agree that Frege's argument fails. However, I will argue against Armstrong's conjecture that numbers simply are such properties as these. I will argue that such properties as being 7-parted are not the numbers themselves, but rather, contain the numbers as constituents.

Similarly, I will agree with Frege that there are such properties as that of having seven instances. However, such properties are not the numbers themselves, but only contain numbers as constituents.

In saying this, I intend to be disagreeing with Frege; yet Frege's own position is subtle, and the nature of my disagreement with Frege is a matter of some delicacy. A close study of Frege may make it seem that I am not disagreeing with him after all. Frege derives his theory of numbers from properties of properties. Yet he did *not* in fact identify the number *n* with the *property* of having *n* instances. Rather, he held that a number is an 'object', and not a 'concept'. A 'concept' is, I take it, something which 'exists' only in the sense of being subject to *second-order* existential quantification (which I will explore later in Chapter 25). A number, however, is something which can be named, and which 'exists' in the sense of being subject to *first-order* existential quantification. What a number is, for Frege, is not the 'concept' corresponding to the second-order predicate 'has *n* instances', but rather, it is an 'object' which is linked in a specifiable way with that 'concept'.

When I talk of universals, what I mean to be talking about are precisely the things Frege calls 'objects'—I mean universals in the sense of recurrences, One Over Many, and not truthmakers or second-order 'beings'. So when I deny that a number is the property of having n instances, I *do* mean to contradict Frege's doctrine that a number is an object which corresponds appropriately to the 'concept' of having n instances.

My main reason for disagreeing with Frege's theory is that I can see something else that numbers might be, something else which can more aptly be identified with natural numbers. What this something else might be, however, I leave for a moment, while I look harder at the Mill–Armstrong theory that number is a property of aggregates. Although I have no direct argument against Frege's theory, I do have an argument against Armstrong's. And the nature of my argument against Armstrong suggests a rival theory to Frege's.

The grid A does have the property of *containing 49 pebbles*. But this property is clearly not itself the number 49, since the number 49 is surely not a property which is specific to *pebbles*. Rather, the property of containing 49 pebbles must be constructed somehow, *using* the number 49 as a constituent.

Armstrong's suggestion, I take it, is that the number 49 is the property of *containing 49 parts*. And therefore, presumably, we should be able to use this property to construct the property of *containing 49 pebbles*. Somehow, we need to be able to put the property of being a pebble together with the property of 49-partedness, to yield the property of containing 49 pebbles. I claim that this cannot be done. Hence, I claim that the number 49 is not the property of 49-partedness.

The reason why 49-partedness cannot be used to construct 'contains 49 pebbles' is this. The latter property applies to an aggregate when the property of 'being a pebble' applies to each of 49 specific parts of it. But the parts to which 'being a pebble' applies must be the very same parts which number 49. It is not enough that the aggregate A be 'a heap of pebbles' (i.e. composed wholly of parts each of which is a pebble) *and* that it be '49–parted'. It could have both *those* properties by containing 49 *rows* of pebbles.

In order to construct 'containing 49 pebbles', we must somehow stick '49-parted' together with 'being a pebble'. But the first of these attaches to the whole heap, whereas the second attaches to things which result from just one particular way among many of dividing the heap into parts.

Here is how 'containing 49 pebbles' must be constructed. We must decompose Armstrong's property of 49-partedness into separate constituents. The property 'being 49-parted' is in fact a complex universal, holding of an aggregate like A when:

> *There are things which number 49 and each is a part of A.*

This begins with a quantifier, 'there are'. The things within the scope of this quantifier are precisely the things to which we need to apply the predicate 'is a pebble'. So the only way to construct the property of 'containing 49 pebbles' is by adding an extra conjunct *within the scope of that quantifier*. When we do that, we obtain the following analysis of the property of containing 49 pebbles:

> 'A contains 49 pebbles' is true just when:
> *There are things, which number 49, and each of these is a part of A, and each of these is a pebble.*

Under this analysis, Armstrong's property of 49-partedness has fallen into pieces. The number 49 was not that property itself; rather, it occurs somewhere among the pieces.

In a similar manner, I argue, Frege's property of 'having *n* instances' should not be taken as a simple, unanalysed property, but should be constructed out of simpler constituents, the number *n* itself being numbered among those constituents. The analysis should be along the lines:

> 'P has *n* instances' is true just when:
> *There are things which number n, and each of these instantiates P.*

I cannot argue for this analysis in quite the same way that I have argued against Armstrong. Against Armstrong I complain that, in trying to analyse

> A contains 49 pebbles,

there is no way we can link the two properties 'is a pebble' and 'is 49-parted' in order to yield the proposition in question.

Yet I cannot make the analogous complaint against Frege. I cannot complain that, in trying to analyse

> A contains 49 pebbles,

there is no way we can link the two properties 'is a pebble' and 'has 49 instances' in order to yield the proposition in question. We can conjoin 'is a pebble' to 'is part of A'. Then we can stick the resulting conjunctive property together with the Fregean second-order property, to yield:

'A contains 49 pebbles' is true just when:
Being a pebble and being in A instantiates *has 49 instances.*

No problem faces this analysis, analogous to the problem facing Armstrong when he tries to stick together the two properties of *n*-partedness and pebblehood.

The reason for the disanalogy between Armstrong's problems and Frege's is that Armstrong must face the fact that aggregates can be divided into parts in many alternative ways. A property, in contrast, cannot be supplied with instances in many alternative ways. It has the instances it has, and that's that.

Properties are, in this way, like *sets* rather than aggregates. An aggregate can be broken into parts in many ways, but a set has the members it has, and that's that. Presenting us with a set determines unambiguously what its members are, so there is a unique answer to the question how many members it has.

Hence, if we transpose Armstrong's aggregate theory into a set theory, my argument against Armstrong will lapse. The transposed theory would identify the number *n* with the property of *having n members*. There would then be no problem about analysing the claim that a set C *contains n pebbles*. We can simply conjoin the attribution of the number *n* to the set, with the attribution of being a pebble to each of its members:

'C is a set of *n* pebbles' is true just when:
C has the number-property n and for any member x of C, x is a pebble.

This analysis escapes my objection to Armstrong. And yet I urge a competing analysis of the form:

'C is a set of *n* pebbles' is true just when:
There are things, which number n, and each of these is a member of C, and each of these is a pebble.

I confess, then, that my argument against the aggregate theory of number does not carry over into an analogous argument against the theory that number is a property of *properties*; nor into an argument against the theory that number is a property of *sets*.

Nevertheless, it is surely plausible that there is a strong analogy among the properties:

having *n* parts,
having *n* instances,
having *n* members.

I have argued that the first of these must be analysed in a way which yields the number *n* itself as just one of its constituents. This at least makes it more plausible to suggest that the same thing holds also for the other two properties. The number *n*, then, is *not* the property of having *n* parts, *nor* is it the property of 'having *n* instances', nor of 'having *n* members'. Rather, it is something simpler which occurs as a common constituent in all three of these properties.

The analysis I suggest for these three properties has a uniform structure, and will take the following form:

$$\text{`X} \begin{cases} \text{has } n \text{ parts} \\ \text{has } n \text{ instances} \\ \text{has } n \text{ members} \end{cases} \text{' is true just when:}$$

There are things which number n, and each of these is

$$\begin{cases} \text{a part of X} \\ \text{an instance of X} \\ \text{a member of X} \end{cases}.$$

The central problem I face, then, is that of explaining more fully just what sort of universal a number *is*—just what sort of universal corresponds to the form of words: 'There are things which number *n*.'

But before expounding my own theory, I will take stock of an alternative and widely held theory. This alternative theory agrees that the number *n* is indeed a common constituent of the three properties I have canvassed, but it holds that that common constituent is not a universal at all but an abstract individual.

5   Numbers as Paradigms

I HAVE argued that the number n should not be identified with any of the properties,

> has n parts,
> has n instances,
> has n members,

but rather, should be construed as a common constituent in each of these three properties.

So far, what I am claiming is in agreement with a kind of theory that I do not accept, yet which is so elegant that it has become the orthodoxy among the mathematicians of our times. I deny that a number is a property of an aggregate, *or* of a property, *or* of a set; and *so far* I am in agreement with mathematical orthodoxy. Where I part company is over my claim that, nevertheless, numbers are universals—even though they are not any of the universals canvassed so far, they are nevertheless universals of some different sort.

Mathematical orthodoxy, in contrast, takes numbers not to be universals at all. Consider for instance the following theory. Suppose some particular entity is chosen, say a particular n-membered set, and that this entity is arbitrarily designated as being 'the number n'. Next, suppose some particular relational predicate is selected, say:

> '. . . has members which stand in a one-to-one correlation with the members of . . .'.

The designated entity n may then be used to fill one of the two empty slots in the chosen relation, to yield the *property*:

> '. . . has members which stand in a one-to-one correlation with the members of n'.

This property holds of any n-membered set, and of nothing else.

The most appealing version of this strategy is that of von Neumann; see for instance Halmos (1960, s. II). Each natural number is identified with a particular paradigm n-membered set: the set of its predecessors. The number 2 for instance is the two-membered set $\{1,0\}$. The number 1 is the one-membered set $\{0\}$. And even the number zero is the set of its predecessors; having no predecessors, zero is just the empty set.

I think this theory of numbers is magnificent. It is interesting to note a close resemblance between this theory of numbers, and a traditional, nominalist solution to the problem of universals. Nominalists, like Berkeley, especially in the Introduction, to his *Principles of Human Knowledge* (see Armstrong, 1965), have sometimes argued as follows. There is no *one* thing which, say, all horses have in common. Rather, each horse *resembles* some particular, paradigm horse. Russell complained, in *The Problems of Philosophy* (1912, ch. 9), that this theory does nevertheless admit *one* universal at least, namely *resemblance*. If nominalists are to rebut Russell's complaint, they must argue that there is no One Over Many called 'resemblance'; rather, there is just a primitive predication of particular resemblances. If resemblance itself is said to 'exist' at all, this must only be in the sense of being subject to higher-order quantification—'Black Ben resembles Dobbin' entails at most that 'There is somehow that Black Ben is to Dobbin', but not that 'There is something that is somehow to Black Ben and Dobbin'.

Similar remarks carry over to the von Neumann theory of numbers. Just as problems in the theory of universals have driven nominalists to their theory, so too problems in the theory of sets have drawn mathematicians towards theories of von Neumann's sort.

Frege and Russell began with the idea of a number n being the property which a *property* has when it has n instances. But properties came to be conflated with sets. So the Frege–Russell theory became, first, that the number n is the property a set has when it has n members; and then second, this property of sets, being itself a property after all, became conflated with a set of sets. The number n thus became *the set of all n-membered sets*.

And yet arguments deriving from Cantor have convinced us that *there can be no set of all n-membered sets*. Any set is a member of n-membered sets which aren't members of it. To suppose otherwise lands us in contradictions.

In response to this, what the von Neumann theory does is to abandon the attempt to treat a number as a One Over Many, to pick instead some *paradigm n*-membered set, and to call any set n-membered if it '*resembles*' this paradigm. The 'resemblance' required here involves a complex sort of higher-order predication. But this higher-order predication cannot be taken to correspond to a universal in the sense of a One Over Many. That is, a predicate like 'stands in some one-to-one correlation with' cannot correspond to some set containing all and only the pairs $\langle x,y \rangle$ for which the members of x can be correlated one-to-one with the members of y. If we *were* to posit such a set of pairs, then we would land in precisely the contradictions which Cantor elicits from the Frege–Russell theory, and which deflected us in von Neumann's direction in the first place.

Some set theories manage to avoid contradictions, even though they allow some sort of set-theoretical counterpart for a predicate like 'stands in some one-to-one correlation with'. Such theories suppose there to be something called a *proper class* containing all and only the pairs $\langle x,y \rangle$ for which the members of x can be correlated one-to-one with the members of y. See for instance Lemmon (1969). The key characteristic of a proper class is that it is not a member of any set or class at all. If 'having a property' is to go hand in hand with 'belonging to a set or proper class', then proper classes cannot be construed as having any properties at all. The nature of proper classes is, in fact, altogether perplexing. For this reason, it is something of a comfort to rescue natural numbers from that realm of proper classes, and to make them plain, down-to-earth sets. Something has to remain in the realm of proper classes; but it is better that the relation of 'one-to-one correlability' should remain there than that the dear old natural numbers should do so.

In developing a theory of numbers, von Neumann's is clearly 'the one to beat'. But I will not try to show what is wrong with von Neumann's theory. The things he calls numbers may exist all right; and he is entitled to call them 'numbers'. I will argue only that there are other things as well, which I am equally entitled to call 'numbers'. And although it is often futile to dispute about which concepts are 'more basic' than which others, when they are interdefinable, nevertheless, I do think of the things I call numbers as being more basic than von Neumann's 'numbers'. The things I call numbers will, in fact, enter into the explanation of *why* von Neumann's predication, 'is one-to-one correlable with n', applies to n-membered sets and nothing else.

6   Numbers as Relations

NUMBERS figure importantly in empirical assertions concerning contingent beings, like our possessions, our enemies, our friends, square grids of pebbles, and so forth. For instance we say things of the form:

(a) The number of F's is at least three.

(Or more naturally perhaps, 'There are at least three F's').

Many such numerical assertions are logically equivalent to assertions in which no numerals appear. For instance, the assertion that there are at least three F's is logically equivalent to:

(b) $\forall x \forall y \exists z. (x \neq z \ \& \ y \neq z \ \& \ Fz)$.

(Assuming we interpret (a) and (b) in non-empty domains, any interpretation under which one of these is true must be an interpretation under which the other is true too.)

Analogously, 'There are at least four F's' will be logically equivalent to:

$\forall w \forall x \forall y \exists z. (w \neq z \ \& \ x \neq z \ \& \ y \neq z \ \& \ Fz)$.

For every natural number n, there will be a logical equivalence between 'There are at least n F's' and a formula of this format. For $n = 1$, we will have 'There is at least one F' coming out as equivalent to:

$\exists z.Fz$.

This scheme generalizes down to $n = 1$; but it does not generalize down to $n = 0$. Initially, I found this disquieting, since it seemed to betray some shortcoming in the scheme of translation for number-statements. But then, I thought, perhaps zero is simply a special case?

However, there is a better explanation of why the scheme does not generalize neatly down to zero. The assertion,

The number of F's is zero,

does not, in fact, mean

There are at least zero F's.

Rather, it means

There are at most zero F's.

And how are we to analyse assertions of the form

There are at most n F's?

The natural analysis is that each such assertion is logically equivalent to:

There are *not* at least $(n + 1)$ F's.

Hence the assertion that there are zero F's is logically equivalent to the *denial* that there is at least one F:

$\sim \exists \ z.Fz.$

And this yields the obvious logical equivalent for 'The number of F's is zero'.

The scheme of translation illustrated by (a)–(b) is an unusually concise one. (I learned it from David Lewis.) As n increases, the length of the 'numberless' paraphrase for 'There are at least n F's' will grow *linearly*, by the insertion, at each step, of just one more quantifier.

'$(\forall \ \ldots)$'

and a single additional conjunct

'$\ldots \ \& \ (\ldots \ \ne z) \ \ldots$'

Yet, although concise, this scheme is unintuitive. It is not easy to see that (b) is logically equivalent to (a). There are other, more easily graspable schemes for paraphrasing number-statements, although these alternatives are more prolix, and grow quadratically in length as the number n increases. The most natural equivalent for (a) would probably be:

(c) $\exists x \ \exists y \ \exists z. \ (x \ne y \ \& \ x \ne z \ \& \ y \ne z \ \& \ Fx \ \& \ Fy \ \& \ Fz).$

Given a logical equivalent between (a) and (b) or (c), there remains the question of what philosophical moral, if any, should be drawn from this. Nominalists argue: the truth of (c) does not assert the existence of any such thing as a number; (a) is logically equivalent to (c); therefore, despite appearances, the truth of (a) does not require the existence of any such thing as a number. According to nominalists, there are really no such things as numbers.

Consider, however, the following counter-argument. The truth of (a) *does* require the existence of a number; (b) and (c) are logically equivalent to (a); therefore, despite appearances, the truth of (b) and (c) *does* require the existence of a number.

This latter sort of argument can in fact be deployed to epistemological ends. Suppose we had some idea of how we can come to know the truth of quantificational claims like (b) or (c). Whatever account could be given of our knowledge of (b) or (c) could then be used to account for our knowledge of (a). We can know (a) because we know (b) or (c), and (a) is either identical with, or at least deducible from, (b) or (c). And so this provides us with at least the beginnings of an answer to those who have wondered how we could ever know anything about numbers, if numbers are not the sorts of things we can see or poke.

So by itself, the logical equivalence of (a) with (b) or (c) yields an argument neither for nor against the existence of numbers. It can be used as one of the steps in an argument either way.

Which direction of argument is better motivated? There is a general principle called Ockham's razor, according to which (roughly), the less you believe in, the more rational you are—other things being equal. And this would seem to weigh, of course, in favour of arguing from the 'numberlessness' of (b) or (c) to the 'numberlessness' of (a).

And yet, I claim, there are other considerations which weigh, independently, in favour of numbers. These ensure that 'other things' are not equal, and that even if Ockham does provide an initial presumption against numbers, this is outweighed by other factors.

Number-words occur in statements of the form of (a), which are equivalent to apparently numberless quantificational statements like (b) or (c). Yet number-words also occur in statements of various other sorts, for which it is not at all easy to find even *apparently* numberless logical equivalents.

One classic stumbling-block for the nominalist programme has been the difficulty of finding appropriate paraphrases for statements like,

> (d) The number of the Apostles is equal to the number of the Muses.

This seems to assert that *there is* a number, which the Apostles share with the Muses. But it does not specify which number this is. So there is no specific number of quantifiers and non-identities ($x \neq y$) which are determined by (d); and this gums up attempts to replace the numerical terms in (d) by quantifiers and non-identities, in the manner we did for (a).

Another class of problems for the nominalist stems from the striking fact that *we can count numbers*. We can say things like,

> (e) There are three natural numbers greater than one but less than five.

I am not going to explain here just *how* we can know, or at least have reasonable beliefs about the truth of something like (e); but however we know it, know it we do. Nominalists are in trouble if they cannot find any apparently numberless equivalent for (e), to serve as (b) or (c) did for (a).

My concern, however, is not to argue that this cannot be done. I suspect that there may indeed be ways in which a nominalist can take honest assertions about numbers, and re-express them in such a way as to conceal effectively any reference to numbers.

This sort of thing can in fact be done more widely. Consider an assertion about me and my full sibling, NSB:

> There are two distinct people, each being a parent of me, and each being a parent of NSB.

This clearly requires the existence of such things as my parents, in addition to myself and my sibling. Yet you can superficially conceal this fact by paraphrasing it into the logically equivalent claim:

> I am a full sibling of NSB.

It is my contention that 'numberless' paraphrases of number-claims are in general precisely like that. The apparently numberless version contains, not a name, but a predicate, or an open sentence, which camouflages reference to numbers.

Look at the equivalence between

> (a) The number of F's is at least three,

and

> (c) $\exists x \, \exists y \, \exists z. \, (x \neq y \, \& \, x \neq z \, \& \, y \neq z \, \& \, Fx \, \& \, Fy \, \& \, Fz)$.

The latter contains no explicit reference to a number; it provides the very best sort of case for a nominalist. It contains no name of any number.

Yet (c) does contain the following open sentence, with three free variables x, y, and z:

> $(x \neq y \, \& \, x \neq z \, \& \, y \neq z)$.

Any open sentence like this, with three free variables, will be true of various *triples* of things. And this open sentence, in particular, will be true of any triple of things which are numerically distinct from one another.

Traditionally, an open sentence with n free variables has been thought to correspond to an *n-place relation*. There are good reasons for resisting the assumption that for every open sentence, there is a corresponding universal (or set). And yet, in some specific cases, it may well be reasonable to conjecture that the reason why an open sentence is true of some triple is that there *is* something which is related to that triple.

I claim that there is indeed something, a universal, which is instantiated by each triple of numerically distinct things. We may call it the relation of *threefold mutual distinctness*. Or, call it the number three.

I claim: any number n is the n-place relation of n-fold mutual distinctness.

The source of numbers, then, is the relation of non-identity, $(x \neq y)$, or, to use a word tracing back to (translations of) Aristotle, *the dyad*. On this account, the natural numbers begin at two: the number two being simply the dyad, the relation of mutual distinctness expressed by the open sentence $(x \neq y)$. The numbers 1 and 0 *can* be introduced in an *ad hoc* way, for instance as the universals corresponding to the following open sentences:

the number one: $(x = x)$ -the property (or relation) of self-identity

or: $\exists \, y.(y = x)$ -the property of being some-thing.

the number zero: $(x \neq x)$ -the property (or relation) of non-self-identity,

or: $\forall \, y.(y \neq x)$ -the property of not being anything.

We can thus construct relatively plausible candidates for zero and one, but however convenient this may be, it is somewhat artificial. And I do not mind this artificiality. The *natural* numbers, I claim, do start at two. The *integers* (signed numbers) are something altogether different: I will treat them as merely a special case of the *real numbers*. And the integers do include zero and one in a non-artificial manner. But the natural numbers don't.

Natural numbers, then, are relations of mutual distinctness. When we meet with small collections of things of certain given sorts, it is sometimes possible to *see* or *feel* that they have something in common. Small numbers are universals which are as immediately 'perceptible' as any universals are, or indeed, as anything is. Think of shape, for instance, as an example of a universal which, plausibly, can be directly perceived. Perception of number would seem to be presupposed in many cases of perception of shape, for instance in perceiving the difference in shape between a pentagon and a hexagon. If you believe in any universals at all, then it is plausible to suggest in particular that there is a universal – there is something in common—between for instance the following arrays of x's and o's.

```
  ×       ×         0        0
      ×                 0
  ×       ×         0        0
```

Any five things arrayed thus are said to be a *quincunx*; the universal involved is striking enough to have been given a name, and to be recognized as the same whether the five things be trees, fountains, lanterns, spots on a die, or whatever. The property (or relation) of being a quincunx is in fact a complex universal, including spatial relations as well as number; but *being five* is at least one of the constituents of this clearly perceptible universal.

It is important to recognize that I am identifying a number with a relation among several things, and *not* with a property of an aggregate. Frege's objections to Mill, and mine to Armstrong, are objections to taking numbers to be properties. They do not apply to a theory which identifies numbers with *relations among* the things which constitute an aggregate.

As Frege might point out, when you ask 'How many?' and point for instance at the contents of this box:

```
┌─────────────────────────┐
│                         │
│        hot shot         │
│                         │
└─────────────────────────┘
```

you could get the answer 'Two words', or 'Seven letters' (meaning letter-*tokens*, inscriptions), or 'Four letters' (meaning letter-*types*, items in the English alphabet). What is in the box has the property of having two parts, each of which is a word. It also has the property of having seven parts, each of which is a distinct inscription of a letter. It also has the property of having four parts, each of which is an inscription of a different letter. But *it*, what is in the box, the only number *it* has is the number *one*. The words 'hot' and 'shot', however, are non-identical; *they* have the number *two*. And so on.

Russell once noted a respect in which numbers seem not to be universals like others. When we say Tom, Dick, and Harry are three fine men, we mean that each is fine, but not that each is three. It has been customary to conclude that what is three cannot be the individuals, but rather, is something like the set containing all three of them. Yet this conclusion is not forced on us if we allow that numbers might be relations rather than properties. Tom, Dick, and Harry may be three, without each being three, for the same sort of reason that four propositions may be mutually inconsistent, without each one being inconsistent.

7   Numbering Sets

I HAVE argued that a natural number is a relation of mutual distinctness. It is instructive to see what becomes of this theory if we interpret relations set-theoretically, in the customary contemporary manner, as classes of ordered n-tuples. From a set-theoretical perspective, an open sentence with n free variables corresponds to a class, called its extension, containing all and only those ordered n-tuples of which that open sentence is true.

From such a set-theoretical perspective, my theory would become this: the number 3 is the relation of threefold mutual distinctness. And set-theoretically, a relation is a set of ordered pairs. Thus, on a set-theoretical version of my theory, the number 3 would be the extension of the open sentence $(x \neq y \,\&\, x \neq z \,\&\, y \neq z)$, which is to say the number 3 is the class:

$$3 = \{\langle a, b, c \rangle : a \neq b \,\&\, a \neq c \,\&\, b \neq c\},$$

the class of all ordered triples of distinct things.

Compare this with the Russell version of Frege's theory: the number 3 is the class of all three-membered sets:

$$3 = \{\{a, b, c\} : a \neq b \,\&\, a \neq c \,\&\, b \neq c\}.$$

There is an obvious isomorphism between my referents for numerals, and Russell's. With appropriate safeguards against Russell's contradiction, Russell's theory manages to capture all the important strutural interrelationships among numbers—as captured for instance in the Peano axioms. So, in virtue of the obvious isomorphism between his theory and mine, I can be confident that I too can capture all the important mathematical structure described by the Peano axioms.

Yet there is an important problem with the Russell theory. Remember that there is no set of all sets. Similarly, there can be no set of all three-membered sets. And this is awkward, to say the least, for a theory which sets out to identify the number three with the set of all three-membered sets.

Russell opted for a theory in which there are many different sets, each of which counts as *a* number three. There is, first, the set of all three-membered sets *whose members are all non-sets*. This is the first number three. The second number three will be: The set of all three-membered sets whose members are *sets of non-sets*. And so on up through sets of sets of . . . of non-sets.

In effect, for Russell there is a property of being a three-membered set of non-sets; and there is a property of being a three-membered set of sets of non-sets; and so on. But there is no single property which is shared by three-membered sets of non-sets *and* by three-membered sets of sets of non-sets.

This hierarchical picture can be subjected to a variety of modifications. But, in whatever form, a hierarchy of threes has been widely felt to be unsatisfactory. It has proved more pleasing to identify the number three with some single, paradigm three-membered set, in the manner of von Neumann.

In the light of this, I wish to clarify the theory I am proposing. I am not defending the view that a number is a set: I am arguing neither that a number is a set of n-membered sets, nor that it is a paradigm n-membered set. Nor, even, is it a property of n-membered sets. Rather, the number n is a universal which is instantiated by the *members* of any n-membered set. By designating a *universal*, of the recurrence or One Over Many sort, as the number n, I can share in many of the advantages the von Neumann theory has over the Frege–Russell theory. In particular, I can avoid the inconvenience of a hierarchy of rivals for the title of 'the number three'.

The role of set theory, I urge, can be understood in the following way. Set theory should not be seen as explaining what constitutes the numbers. Rather, set theory generates an example, one example among others, of pluralities of things which instantiate the numbers. Consider for instance von Neumann's 'numbers'. His zero is the empty set, Φ; his number one is $\{\Phi\}$; and these are numerically distinct,

$$\Phi \neq \{\Phi\};$$

and hence they instantiate my number two. In a similar way, von Neumann's 0, 1, and 2 instantiate my number three. And so on. If all the sets posited by set theory exist, then all my natural numbers are instantiated. If all these sets exist necessarily, and can be known to exist a priori, then set theory gives arithmetic a necessary, a priori 'foundation'. The truths of arithmetic can be seen as actually true of actual things, without being contingent on experience of empirical reality. Arithmetic is assured of autonomy from the other sciences.

If mathematicians were less concerned with their purity and

autonomy from other sciences, there would be less need to rest so heavily on set theory. Mathematicians should have more faith: *there are* things which instantiate all the important properties and relations of mathematics. Sets provide one example, but there are others: space for instance, or time.

Indeed, as soon as we start introducing a few numbers into our list of existents, the theory of numbers rapidly becomes self-supporting. Suppose there to be *any* two things (other than the number two itself), whose existence and non-identity is given to us: $(a \neq b)$. Then there is, I claim, a universal which they instantiate—the number two. Now count how many things there are:

$$(a \neq b) \ \& \ (a \neq 2) \ \& \ (b \neq 2).$$

So the number three is instantiated. By following this method, we will find that all the numbers are instantiated.

Thus, once set theory, or something else, has supplied us with things to be counted, from there on numbers supply their own instantiations.

The role of set theory is not one of explaining what numbers are, but rather, of supplying an extraordinarily fertile source of *instantiations* for numbers. But since numbers instantiate one another, their need for set-theoretical instantiations is only marginal. The more important role set theory fills, is that it supplies instantiations, not only for natural numbers, but also for all, or nearly all, of the other structures mathematicians have wanted to study. This role, of supplying instantiations, was once played mainly by *space*, or by space and time, or space-time. But truths about space-time have been contaminated by worries from physics. Set theory is supposed to be uncontaminated by any hint of contingency, and that is why it is so important for mathematics.

8   Approximations

CONSIDER again the Pebble proof that $n^2 \neq 2m^2$ (see Fig. 9). If A were to be equal to B and C, then a would have to be equal to b and c.

Yet for the same reason if A were *greater* than B and C, then a would have to be *less* than b and c. And conversely if A were less than B and C, then a would have to be greater than b and c.

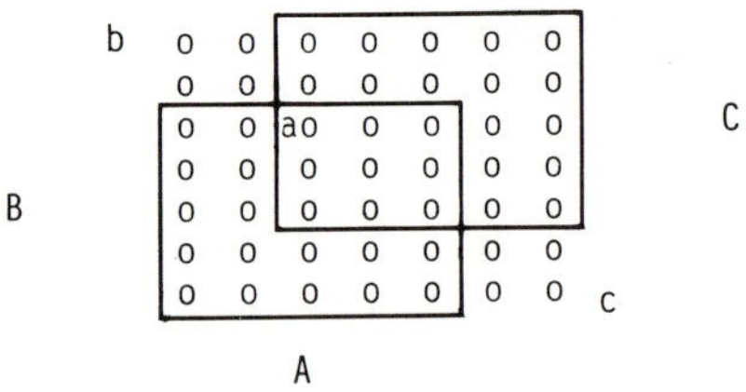

```
 b  o  o │ o  o  o  o  o
    o  o │ o  o  o  o  o
    ┌─────────────┐
    o  o │ao  o  o │ o  o        C
    o  o │ o  o  o │ o  o
 B  o  o │ o  o  o │ o  o
    └─────────────┘
    o  o  o  o  o │ o  o
    o  o  o  o  o │ o  o  o
                            c
         A
```

FIG. 9

Indeed, if A were some particular number, *x* say, *greater* than B and C, then a would have to be just that number *less* than b and c—and conversely. This can be seen from the diagram. Suppose we begin with the two squares B and C, and we set out to rearrange them to form square A. We begin by placing B and C exactly as in the diagram, with the pebbles doubled up on square a (see Fig. 10). To construct square A, we will need to take one from each pair in square a, and place it in b or c.

Suppose then that a contains *x more* pairs than there are empty places in b and c. Then we will have x pebbles left over after we have completed square A. This means B and C contained *x more* than A.

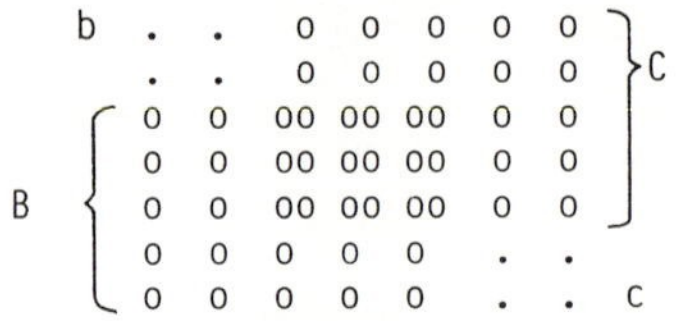

```
 b  .  .   o  o  o  o  o  ⎫
    .  .   o  o  o  o  o  ⎬ C
  ⎡ o  o  00 00 00  o  o  ⎭
  ⎢ o  o  00 00 00  o  o
 B ⎨ o  o  00 00 00  o  o
  ⎢ o  o  o  o  o   .  .
  ⎣ o  o  o  o  o   .  .  c
```

FIG. 10

Suppose conversely that a contained *x fewer* pairs than there were empty spaces in b and c. Then, after we had finished taking one from each pair in a, we would still be *x* pebbles short of completing square A. This means that B and C would contain *x fewer* than A.

There is an algebraic counterpart to this reasoning. It can be proved that if

$$n^2 = 2m^2 + x$$

then

$$
\begin{aligned}
(n + 2m)^2 &= n^2 + 4nm + 4m^2 \\
&= n^2 + 4nm + (2m^2 + 2m^2) + (x - x) \\
&= n^2 + (2m^2 + x) + 4nm + 2m^2 - x \\
&= n^2 + (n^2) + 4nm + 2m^2 - x \\
&\quad \text{(using the equality } 2m^2 + x = n^2) \\
&= 2n^2 + 4nm + 2m^2 - x \\
&= 2(n + m)^2 - x
\end{aligned}
$$

That is,

if $n^2 = 2m^2 + x$
then $(n + 2m)^2 = 2(n + m)^2 - x$.

And conversely, it can be shown that:

if $n^2 = 2m^2 - x$
then $(n + 2m)^2 = 2(n + m)^2 + x$.

The algebraic proof is neat; but remember that *what* has been proved is a fact *about arrangements of pebbles*. Return therefore to Fig. 10 to check this out! Sure enough, a exceeds b and c by 1, and A falls short of B and C by 1:

$$3^2 = 2(2)^2 + 1$$
$$7^2 = 2(5)^2 - 1.$$

The square A can be constructed using a, b, and c, by lining up a, b, and c corner-to-corner and then completing the square. In the same way, a still larger square, A+ say, could be constructed by lining up A, B, and C corner-to-corner and then completing the square. Similarly, by placing B and A corner-to-corner we may create B+, and by placing C and A corner-to-corner we may create C+ (see Fig. 11). And we can then argue that since A is one *less* than B and C, therefore A+ must be one *more* than B+ and C+. And if we count to make sure, we find that, sure enough,

$$17^2 = 2(12)^2 + 1.$$

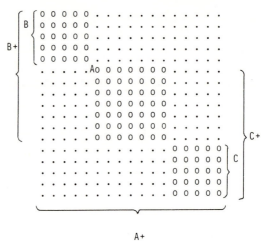

FIG. 11

We can thus contruct a never-ending chain of squares, each one differing by *just one* from two equal smaller squares:

$8 = 2^2 + 2^2$, which is one *less* than $9 = 3^2$

$50 = 5^2 + 5^2$, which is one *more* than $49 = 7^2$

$288 = 12^2 + 12^2$, which is one *less* than $289 = 17^2$.

From this we may extract the sequence of number-pairs which the Greeks called 'side' and 'diagonal' numbers (see Fig. 12).

The fraction D_j/S_j gives a closer and closer approximation to $\sqrt{2}$, as j increases. The fraction $3/2 = 1.5$, which is greater than $\sqrt{2}$; and $7/5 = 1.40$, which is less than $\sqrt{2}$; and $17/12 = 1.4166$, which is greater than $\sqrt{2}$ but getting nearer, and so on.

But wait a moment. In what sense *are* we 'getting closer and closer to $\sqrt{2}$'? What is this thing $\sqrt{2}$, which we are supposedly getting closer and closer to?

What does it mean to say that $41/29$ is closer to $\sqrt{2}$ than $17/12$ is? The numbers 41 and 29, 17 and 12, were constructed in such a way that, in both cases, the square of the larger differs by just one from two squares of the smaller. Thus, the square of side 41, and the square of side 17 *both* differ from two smaller squares by precisely the same amount—by one! So the square of side 41 is *no closer* than the square of side 17 to equalling two smaller equal squares!

Pebble Pythagoras gives us no reason at all to think there is any such

Side numbers	Diagonal numbers
2	3
5	7
12	17
29	41
.	.
.	.
.	.
S_j	D_j
$S_{j+1} = S_j + D_j$	$D_{j+1} = 2S_j + D_j$
.	.
.	.
.	.

FIG. 12

thing as $\sqrt{2}$ for the side and diagonal numbers to approximate. Quite the reverse. It *seems* to show that there are *no numbers* for which $n^2 = 2m^2$.

The sense in which D_j/S_j 'approaches $\sqrt{2}$', as j increases, is this. As j increases, D_j^2 becomes more and more nearly *twice* S_j^2. The *proportion* or *ratio* between D_j^2 and S_j^2 becomes more and more nearly the proportion $2:1$.

Yet even this does not generate for us any such thing as $\sqrt{2}$, a 'number', whose square *is* 2.

9 Arithmetic and Geometry

When the Greeks discovered the incommensurables like $\sqrt{2}$, what they discovered was more than the arithmetical fact that $n^2 \neq 2m^2$. It was more also than the fact that $D_j^2 = 2S_j^2 \pm 1$. And it was even more than the fact that the squares of diagonal and side numbers stand in proportions which get nearer and nearer to the proportion $2:1$, without ever getting there.

What the Greeks discovered was that *there are* proportions which hold between, for instance, lengths, *but which do not hold between any natural numbers.*

Consider, for instance, the construction of two squares equal in area to a given square, as in Fig. 13. The side of A is incommensurable with the side of B or C: there is no way of choosing a unit length such that the side of A is n of these units long, and the side of B or C is m of these units long.

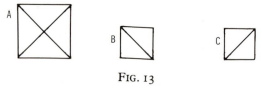

FIG. 13

And yet there is clearly some relationship—a relationship of *proportion*—which holds between these two lengths. The side of A is *longer* than the side of B. But it is *less than twice as long as* the side of B.

If we combine B and C to form a rectangle, D, as in Fig. 14, then the

FIG. 14

proportion between the long side of D and the short side of D is the same as the proportion between the numbers 2 and 1, or 10 and 5, and so on. The long side of D is clearly *twice* the length of the short side, in exactly the way that the number of pebbles in a heap of 10 is *twice* the number in a heap of 5.

Some proportions between lengths, then, are proportions which hold also between numbers. But some proportions between lengths do not hold between any (natural) numbers. And $\sqrt{2}$ is one of those proportions. It is a proportion which is uninstantiated among the natural numbers, but is clearly instantiated in geometry, and is just as clearly instantiated elsewhere too, as for instance by proportions between intervals of time, or velocities, or masses.

I have sometimes wondered whether the Greeks might have first discovered the purely arithmetical fact that $n^2 \neq 2m^2$, and only *later* discovered that there are irrational proportions between magnitudes like length, area, and volume. My Pebble Pythagoras shows that they could have done so. They did not have algebraic notation; but manipulations of pebbles could have mimicked an algebraic proof.

I was somewhat encouraged in my conjecture about the arithmetical origin of the discovery that $n^2 \neq 2m^2$, when I found references to Oskar Becker, who seems to have defended a similar view, for instance in (1957, pp. 40 ff., 51, and 52) and in (1936, pp. 533–53, especially pp. 544 ff.). However, Becker has been severely criticized, for instance by Walter Burkert (1972, especially p. 436), who maintains that the discovery of irrationals came from geometry. A very readable paper by von Fritz, on 'The discovery of the Incommensurables of Hippasos of Metapontum' (1945) argues the same.

Nevertheless, it is important to distinguish two issues. I agree that the discovery that there *are* incommensurables was *not* purely arithmetical; so in one sense 'the discovery of incommensurables' must have come from outside arithmetic, and most likely from geometry. Yet there is also the purely arithmetical fact that $n^2 \neq 2m^2$; and this could have been discovered purely in arithmetic. The Pythagoreans had a powerful religious excuse for spending a great deal of time playing with pebbles, and studying facts about odds and evens, and so forth. The more I have seen of the sorts of facts they discovered about pebbles, the less improbable it becomes that they should have found that no square grid can be twice the size of a smaller square grid.

There are ancient references, for instance in Aristotle, to a Pythagorean proof by way of 'odds and evens', which may have been purely arithmetical. Heath (1921, p. 91), for instance, seems to think that this Pythagorean proof was a version of the usual algebraic proof by *reductio ad absurdum* ('Suppose $\sqrt{2} = a/b$, then . . .'), differing only in that its presentation was free from algebraic notation. Euclid gives a version of an 'odds and evens' proof in the *Elements*, Bk. X, appendix 27 (which is, unfortunately, missing from the Heath translation), though in Euclid's presentation the proof still looks rather geometrical to me.

Still, a thoroughly non-geometrical proof can be given, which is fairly close to Euclid's 'odds and evens' proof, as follows.

Suppose A = B + C and B = C, for three square grids A, B, C (see Fig. 15). And suppose A to be the *smallest* such square. Then the numbers in A and B must be mutually prime (the Pythagoreans knew a lot about primes), or else we would be able to make smaller squares meeting the same conditions, contradicting our supposition that A is the smallest such square.

```
o  o  o  o  o  o
o  o  o  o  o  o
o  o  o  o  o  o        o  o  o  o        o  o  o  o
o  o  o  o  o  o        o  o  o  o        o  o  o  o
o  o  o  o  o  o        o  o  o  o        o  o  o  o
o  o  o  o  o  o        o  o  o  o        o  o  o  o

A                      B                 C
```

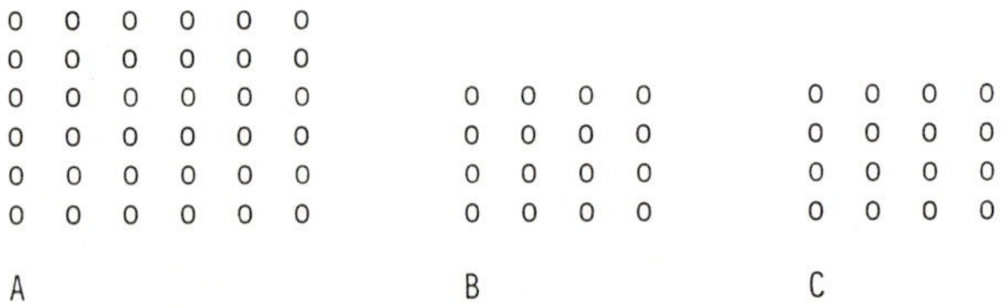

FIG. 15

A and B must be mutually prime. Yet clearly A must be even, since it can be divided into two equal parts B and C. And so, since A is even, and A and B are mutually prime, it follows that B must be odd.

Yet if A is even, then it can be divided into halves, either horizontally or vertically (see Fig. 16). The number of B, being half of A, must equal the number to the left of the vertical line. But the number to the left of the vertical line is clearly even. Yet B is odd. So we have derived the consequence that *an odd number equals an even*

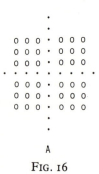

A

FIG. 16

number—which is absurd. And hence we cannot have both that A = B + C and that B = C: which was to be shown.

History aside, however, it remains true that there are two quite distinct facts to be discovered. There is the arithmetical one: that $n^2 \neq 2m^2$ for all natural numbers n and m. And there is the geometrical one: that there are proportions which hold between no two natural numbers.

Arithmetic yields a sequence of pairs of squares, and in each of these pairs, one of the squares differs by just one from being twice the number of the other square. As we choose larger and larger squares, the *proportion* between the paired squares becomes closer and closer to the proportion between 2 and 1. The larger one becomes more and more nearly twice the smaller one. But there are no two natural numbers which, when squared, yield results which stand in the proportion of 2 to 1.

It is important, for my purposes, to note that there are several distinct levels operating in this domain. There are the natural numbers, and there are relationships of proportion which hold between the numbers. The proportion between one number and another may be the same, or greater, or less than the proportion holding between two other numbers. So, for instance, the proportion between 1 and 2 is *closer* to that between 25 and 49 than it is to that between 4 and 9.

Natural numbers, then, instantiate proportions. And proportions are a completely different kettle of fish. Real numbers are proportions: and that is why real numbers are entities of a completely different level from natural numbers. Real numbers emerge as relations among natural numbers, just as natural numbers emerged as relations among individuals. But the discovery of irrational numbers involved the demonstration that there are proportions which are not instantiated by any natural numbers. That discovery had to come from some source outside arithmetic.

10   Proportions

THE notion of *proportion* needs to be explained. Compare the proportion between two numbers, say 3 and 2, with the proportion between the diagonal and side of a square. I said earlier that the fraction 3/2 is greater than root 2: in what sense then is the proportion between 3 and 2 'greater than' the proportion between the diagonal and side of a square?

Consider two particular squares, one of side D and the other of side S, where the area of the first is twice that of the second (so that the side of the first equals the diagonal of the second).

Then consider the two *relations*, 'D shorter than' and 'S shorter than'. These are illustrated in Fig. 17. Notice that we will always have, in such a case as this, that z_1 is shorter than y_1.

Now compare these two relations,

> D shorter than,
> S shorter than,

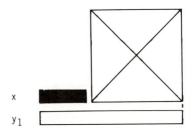

x is D shorter than y_1

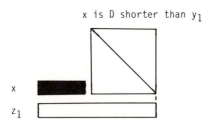

x is S shorter than z_1

FIG. 17

with the two relations,

3 fewer than,
2 fewer than.

Suppose you start with a plurality of things, x, and you apply the relation '3 fewer than', taking you to a plurality y_1. And suppose you start with the same plurality x, and apply the different relation, '2 fewer than', taking you to some plurality z_1. This can be illustrated as in Fig. 18. Notice that we will always have, in such a case, that z_1 are fewer than y_1.

x
```
        o  o  o
        o  o  o
```

y_1
```
        o  o  o
        o  o  o
        o  o  o        x are 3 fewer than y₁
```

z_1
```
        o  o  o  o
        o  o  o  o     x are 2 fewer than z₁.
```

FIG. 18

So compare the two pairs of relations:

D shorter than/S shorter than,
3 fewer than/2 fewer than.

There is a pattern which is common to both (see Fig. 19). So far, then, the relationship between 'D shorter than' and 'S shorter than' is *similar* to that between '3 fewer than' and '2 fewer than'.

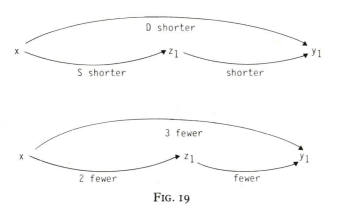

FIG. 19

Now compare what happens when we apply 'D shorter than' or '3 fewer than' twice over, as in Fig. 20. In such a case it is possible that $y_2 = z_3$, in the sense that they are the same, numerically identical collection; but in any case, y_2 must be exactly *as many as* z_3.

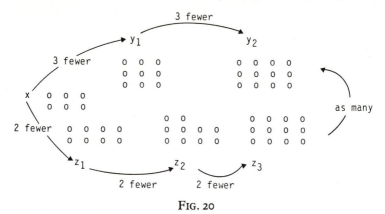

FIG. 20

Compare the numerical case in Fig. 20 with the geometrical case in Fig. 21. In such a case it is *not* possible that $y_2 = z_3$, in the sense that they are the same, numerically identical entities; and in any case, y_2 must be *shorter than* z_3. It is for this reason that the proportion of 3 to 2 is said to be greater than the proportion of D to S (and so greater than root 2).

If we turn from the proportion of 3 to 2, and look next at the proportion of 7 to 5, we will find that the proportion of 7 to 5 is closer to that between D and S. This can be seen from the fact that the results of applying '7 fewer than' *twice over* and '5 fewer than' *three times over*, results in precisely the same structure we obtained for 'D shorter than' and 'S shorter than' (see Fig. 22).

Yet although the proportion of 7 to 5 is closer to that of D to S, it is still not the same; and a difference between them can be elicited by a greater number of repeated applications of the relevant relations. If '7 fewer than' is applied *five* times over, we arrive at the same number we would arrive at by applying '5 fewer than' *seven* times over. This structure is not replicated by repeated applications of the relations 'D shorter than' and 'S shorter than'. Applying 'D shorter than' *five* times over will yield something longer than what we could obtain by applying 'S shorter than' *seven* times over. So the proportion of D to S is greater than that of 7 to 5.

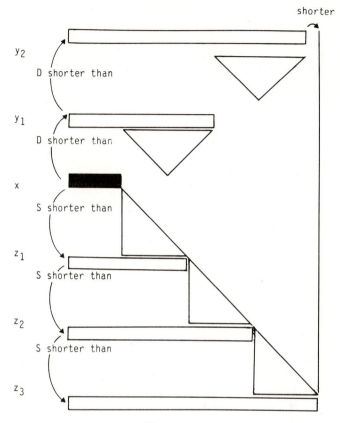

FIG. 21

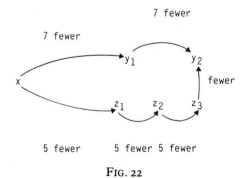

FIG. 22

No matter how many times over we apply the relations 'D shorter than' and 'S shorter than', starting with any given x, we will *never* arrive at a y_m and a z_n of equal length.

In contrast, any two relations 'n fewer than' and 'm fewer than' can *always* be applied to any given plurality x (m times over and n times over, respectively) to yield a y_m and z_n which are equal in number.

This is why the proportion between the diagonal and side of a square is not equal to the proportion between any two natural numbers.

11 Ratios

WHAT is a real number? Newton answered this rather well in his *Arithmetica Universalis* (1728, p. 2): 'By *Number* we understand not so much a Multitude of Unities, as the abstracted Ratio of any Quantity, to another Quantity of the same kind, which we take for Unity.' In other words, real numbers are ratios, or *proportions*. The word 'proportions' is to be preferred in developing a general theory for the following reason. The term 'ratios' is sometimes restricted in its application, so that it is applied to only a subclass of the full class of proportions. On this usage 'ratios' are just those proportions which hold between natural numbers. This subclass of proportions constitutes the set of *rational* numbers.

What are proportions? They are clearly relations of some sort, since they are said to hold between lengths, areas, numbers, and so forth.

But what *sorts* of things do these relationships of proportion hold between? The things they can hold between seem to form a very wide-ranging and heterogeneous collection—lengths, of course, but also masses, temperatures, velocities, numbers, and more things besides. The general term for the sorts of things which can stand in proportions to one another has been: *magnitudes*, or sometimes, *quantities*. And so we need an account of what sort of a thing a magnitude is.

A magnitude is not a physical object. We cannot construe a relation of proportion as holding between physical objects, like metal rods for instance. The lengths of two rods may stand in one proportion, while their volumes stand in a quite different proportion, their masses in another, and so on. A relation of proportion holds, not between objects, but—it would seem—between *properties* of objects, properties like length, mass, and so forth. Proportions, then, are second-order unviersals: they are *relations between universals*.

If proportions are to be relations between *universals*, then it is most natural to construe them as relations between *properties*. Yet it turns out to be easier, at least in the first instance, to treat them as relations between *relations*. Instead of treating proportions as relationships between magnitudes, i.e. properties, I will treat them as relations between *relative magnitudes*, i.e. relations of magnitude, of 'more' or 'less'.

To illustrate, consider lengths, and relative lengths. There have been philosophers who have argued that the status of length, *as a property*, is dubious and derivative. They have argued that properties like length are really best construed as disguised relations; that a thing has no such thing as an intrinsic property of 'being some specific length', but rather, its being a certain length is wholly constituted by its being 'longer than' certain things and 'shorter than' others. The primary universal, on this view, is thus not a magnitude, but the relative magnitudes of 'longer than' and 'shorter than'.

I am not sympathetic to that view. We cannot hastily assume either that length is parasitic on relative length, or that relative length is grounded in intrinsic length. Nevertheless, abstracting from such questions of ontological constitution and epistemological priority— and even from the question whether intrinsic length exists or not—we can nevertheless agree, I think, that *there are* relations of relative length, like 'longer than' and 'shorter than'.

And more specifically, I claim that there are such relations as:

> *so much longer than,*
> *so much shorter than.*

That is to say, we may sometimes say that a is as much longer than b, as c is longer than d. And there are many other such examples of relations of relative magnitude:

> *this much heavier than,*
> *that much faster than,*
> *so many more than;*

and also, there are some further, slightly more 'indefinite' relations of relative magnitude:

> *no more than so much heavier than,*
> *at least this much faster than,*
> etc.

It turns out that these sorts of relations, of relative magnitude, are apt candidates for the role of serving as *the sorts of items between which relations of proportion hold.*

More specifically, it will turn out that the proportions which count as *ratios* can be construed as holding between relations of 'precise' relative magnitude, relations like

> *this much heavier than,* etc.

Proportions which are *not* ratios can be construed as holding between relations of more 'indefinite' relative magnitude, relations like

> *no more than so much heavier than*, etc.

I will explain more fully in due course.

The great advantage of construing proportions as relations between relations is that this makes it possible for us to utilize an already existing, formal theory of real numbers, which I found buried deep in Whitehead and Russell's *Principia Mathematica* (1910–13, vol. 3, pt. VI 'Quantity'). I have also found a closely related theory in untranslated portions of Frege's *Grundgesetze der Arithmetik* (1893–1903, vol. 2, especially ss. 156–64); see also Currie (1986) for discussion and translations of some of the crucial passages.

The formal exposition of Whitehead's theory (Russell attributes the theory to Whitehead in his *Introduction to Mathematical Philosophy* (1919, p. 64)) begins in *Principia Mathematica* section *303 on the theory of ratios. The key definition is the barely intelligible *303.01. Its key feature is this: *ratios are construed as relations between relations.* It may be worth noting that, despite the ferocity of the notation in which it is expressed, Whitehead's theory of fractions was, as Russell says (1919, p. 64), 'specially adapted for their use in measurement'.

On the basis of this account of ratios, an account is then given of real numbers in (roughly) the customary Dedekind manner—real numbers being construed as classes of ratios. This is encapsulated in the mind-boggling propositions *310.01 and *310.011.

But later on, and most interesting of all, comes an alternative construal of real numbers, a construal on which real numbers turn out to be entities of the same logical type as ratios. The trick is roughly this: instead of taking real numbers to be classes of ratios, in the Dedekind manner, we may take them to be unions of those classes which constitute ratios. Real numbers then became classes of just the same sorts of things that ratios are classes of. This is summed up in the totally incomprehensible propositions of *314. The important thing about *314 is this: real numbers and ratios are *both* construed as *relations between relations.*

Whitehead's theory of real numbers would never have come to my notice had it not been for the truly heroic work of Quine. Robert Farrell pointed me to the lucid section 10 of Quine's paper 'Whitehead and the Rise of Modern Logic' (1941). And then I found chapter 6 of Quine's book on *Set Theory and Its Logic* (1969, particularly pp.

129–30). There, Quine not only succinctly reports on Whitehead's theory, but also puts forward his own variant, which contains a minor but interesting improvement: for Whitehead, rational numbers were not themselves real numbers, whereas for Quine rational numbers are simply a proper subset of the real numbers.

The Whitehead theory possesses an extraordinary degree of generality. It applies to almost any kind of relation you can think of. There is a clear indication of this in Quine (1941, pp. 33–4), which I will borrow.

Compare the grandparent relation, call it G, with the great-great-great-grandparent relation, which I will call J. Suppose there are people, x, and a, b, c, d, and z, such that

xGa and aGb and bGc
and cGd and dGz.

Abbreviate this as

xG^5z;

that is let 'xG^5z' mean that there are four things which serve as the links in a chain of five G-relations, leading from x to z.

Whenever xG^5z holds, there will always be someone, e say, such that

xJe and eJz;
abbreviate: xJ^2z.

That is there will always be someone whose great-great-great-grandparent is x, and whose great-great-great-grandchild is z.

In other words, anywhere you can get by five applications of the relation G, you can get by two applications of the relation J. And this implies that anywhere you can get by ten G-steps, you can get by four J-steps; and anywhere you can get by twenty G-steps, you can get by eight J-steps, and so on. A chain of conditions holds:

If xG^5z then xJ^2z
. . . but not xJ^1z or xJ^3z, . . . etc.;
If $xG^{10}z$ then xJ^4z
. . . but not xJ^1z or xJ^2z, . . . etc.;
If $xG^{20}z$ then xJ^8z
. . . but not xJ^1z or xJ^2z, . . . etc.

As an initial proposal (not quite Whitehead's theory), we may say that *whenever any two relations G and J satisfy a chain of conditions of that form, then G stands to J in the ratio 2 : 5.*

That is the ratio $2:5$ is a relationship which holds between two relationships, G and J, if and only if the above chain of conditions holds.

And the rational number, or fraction 2/5, is to be identified with precisely that relation between relations.

Negative numbers emerge very neatly. The ratio *minus two-fifths* holds between any two relations, R and S say, if and only if:

> anywhere you can get *to* by five applications of R, you can get *from* by two applications of S.

In other words, the ratio of minus two-fifths holds between R and S when a chain of conditions of the following form holds:

> If xR^5z, then zS^2x, . . .
> If $xR^{10}z$, then zS^4x, . . . etc.

And so, for instance, the ratio of minus two-fifths will hold between the grand*parent* relation and the great-great-great-grand*child* relation.

This sketch of the theory stands in need of many refinements. I will mention just one. In my exposition so far, I have explained ratios by appeal to *universal* claims of the following general sort:

> For any x and z, if xR^5z, then xS^2z.

There is a technical shortcoming of such universal claims. Suppose we were to meet with a case in which there are no x and y for which xR^5y. In that case, the crucial universal claim turns out to be vacuously true.

In order to forestall that shortcoming, it may be wise to rephrase the theory, replacing the problematic *universal* claims by *existential* ones:

> There is an x and a z such that xR^5z and xS^2z.

And this brings us another step closer to the specific formulation given by Whitehead or Quine.

I pass over further worries about fine-tuning the theory in order to focus on some deeper aspects of the theory.

12   Real Numbers

Norbert Wiener (1912–14) has suggested an alternative version of Whitehead's theory, a version which promises to give it wider applicability. In addition, there is a degree to which Wiener's version seems more intuitively graspable, more satisfying, than Whitehead and Quine's versions.

Suppose we are dealing with a magnitude which has some upper limit, loudness perhaps. Consider then a relation of the form 'this much louder than', and a relation S of the form 'that much louder than'. Suppose we wish to say that there is a ratio of, say, twelve-thirteenths holding between R and S—that R stands to S in the ratio of 12 to 13.

In such a case, will we be happy to say that, if we were to apply R thirteen times over, then we would reach the same result that we would reach by applying S twelve times over? Not really. If we start with some sound x, even a very quiet one, and try to apply the relation R thirteen times over, we may find that we run out of sounds well before we have reached the thirteenth application. How then are we to construe the claim that R and S stand in the proportion 12 : 13? Whitehead's theory fails us.

Wiener suggests an alternative approach. He suggests that we should say that a ratio of 12 : 13 holds between R and S just when *there is some other relationship*, μ, which can serve as a 'common measure' for R and S. Suppose that there is somewhere you can get in one R-step, and you can also get there in twelve μ-steps; and there is somewhere you can get in one S-step, and you can also get there in thirteen μ-steps. Wiener suggests that, under these circumstances, we can say that a ratio of 12 : 13 holds between R and S—even if the Whitehead conditions fail to hold for R and S.

As a first approximation then, following Wiener, we may say that R stands to S in the ratio of 12 to 13, when:

> There is some relation μ such that, for some w, x, y, z: wRx and $w\mu^{12}x$; and ySz and $y\mu^{13}z$.

This theory offers endless scope for fine-tuning, for varying the ordering or scope of the quantifiers, and so forth. But there is a more urgent question to be faced first. The question is, whether any such theory can be developed in a natural way, so as to yield a fully general theory of real numbers, a theory covering irrational proportions as well as ratios.

Initially, it may seem that the Wiener theory could not be extended to cover irrational proportions. After all, the Wiener theory appeals to a relation μ which serves in effect as a *common measure* for R and S. Yet if R and S are incommensurable, then it would seem that there will be no such common measure.

Consider again the irrational proportion between diagonal and side of a square. In particular, consider the relations 'D shorter than' and 'S shorter than' discussed earlier, where D is the side of some specific square, and S is the side of a square of half the area (see Fig. 23). There is no relation μ of the sort

μ = this-much shorter than

such that μ forms a common measure for D and S. That is, for *no such* μ do we have

wDx and $w\mu^n x$,
ySz and $y\mu^m z$,

no matter which natural numbers you choose for n and m, or which things you choose as w, x, y and z.

D   S

FIG. 23

The way to bypass this difficulty is by mobilizing a different, somewhat less precise sort of relation. Consider for instance the following relationship. Suppose there is some specific triangle, EMU (as in Fig. 24).

FIG. 24

Consider then the relation

μ = *no more than MU shorter than*.

(See Fig. 25.)

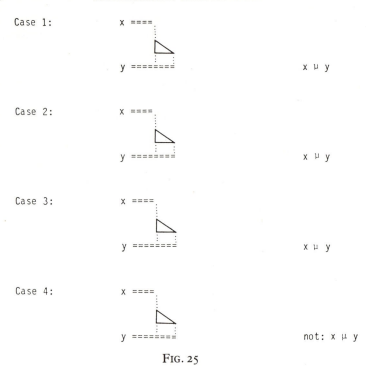

FIG. 25

Using relations μ, of *this* sort, we *can* establish a chain of conditions linking the two 'incommensurable' magnitudes D and S.

Take any pair of 'side' and 'diagonal' numbers, as constructed in Chapter 18, say the side number 2 and diagonal number 3. The fraction 3/2 is larger than $\sqrt{2}$. So consider a length d which divides S evenly in half. Taking three of these lengths will give us something longer than D (see Fig. 26). Let δ be the relation, *no more than d shorter than*; then we will have

> For some w, x, y, z,
> wSx and $w\delta^2 x$,
> yDz and $y\delta^3 z$.

If we take the next pair of diagonal and side numbers, 5 and 7, the situation is slightly different. Whereas 3/2 is *larger* than $\sqrt{2}$, 7/5 is *less* than $\sqrt{2}$. So consider a length which divides S evenly into five parts. Taking seven of these lengths will give us something shorter than D. Hence, conversely, take a length, d′ say, which divides D evenly into

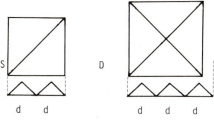

FIG. 26

seven parts; then taking five of these lengths will give us something longer than S (see Fig. 27). Let δ' be the relation, *no more than d' shorter than*; then we will have,

For some w, x, y, z,
wSx and $w\delta'^5x$,
yDz and $y\delta'^7z$.

By this means we can build up a chain of conditions of the form:

For some w, x, y, z,
wSx and $w\delta'^nx$,
yDz and $y\delta'^mz$,

where n and m are any two side and diagonal numbers, respectively.

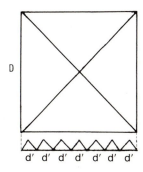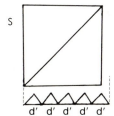

FIG. 27

My theory of real numbers, then, is this. There is a relationship of proportion between D and S; and this proportion holds between any two relationships if and only if a chain of conditions holds, having the form outlined above.

Note that I am not *identifying* a proportion with an infinite chain of conditions. Rather, I am claiming that the proportion $\sqrt{2}$ is the relationship which is instantiated if and only if this chain of conditions holds. But it could equally well be characterized as the relationship which is instantiated if and only if certain *other* chains of conditions hold. The chain of diagonal and side numbers provides just one among many possible sequences 'approximating $\sqrt{2}$'.

My claim is that the various sequences of conditions hold because the proportion is instantiated, but they are not identical with that relationship of proportion. They are merely used to secure unique reference to that proportion in a manner analogous to that in which we can point to *effects* in order to secure reference to their *cause*.

The resulting theory of proportions is a variant of the magnificent achievement, attributed to Eudoxus, and reported in Euclid's *Elements*, Bk. V, definition 5 (see Heiberg and Menge, 1883–1916):

Magnitudes are said to *be in the same ratio*, the first to the second and the third to the fourth, when, if any equimultiples whatever be taken of the first and third, and any equimultiples whatever of the second and fourth, the former equimultiples alike exceed, are alike equal to, or alike fall short of, the latter equimultiples respectively taken in corresponding order.

Eudoxus' theory is closer to Whitehead's than Wiener's. And it does not explicitly commit itself to my account of magnitudes in terms of relations. Yet there is nevertheless a close kinship between Eudoxus' theory, and my theory of proportions as relations between relations.

Eudoxus did not think of ratios or proportions as 'numbers'. On my account, they are indeed quite different sorts of things from the *natural numbers*. Yet proportions are, I claim, numbers of a different sort: real numbers. As Leonard Euler said, in his *Elements of Algebra* (see Hewlett, 1822, pp. 2–3).

Mathematics, in general, is the *science of quantity*; or, the science which investigates the means of measuring quantity. . . . Now we cannot measure or determine any quantity, except by considering some other quantity of the same kind as known, and pointing out their mutual relation. . . . [Thus] a number is nothing but the proportion of one magnitude to another arbitrarily assumed as the unit.

II(c) COMPLEX NUMBERS

13 Imaginary Numbers

'THERE is no fraction whose square is 2, so the square root of 2 is not a fraction.'

'There is no (positive or negative) real number whose square is -1, so the square root of -1 is not a (positive or negative) real number.'

These two inferences are, superficially, closely analogous. Both cases rest on a tacit, existential presupposition: that *there is* something whose square is 2, or -1, respectively.

In the first case, however, the case of real numbers, we can ground the relevant existential presupposition in theorems of geometry. There is a relationship, a proportion, which holds between the diagonal and side of a square; and the existence of this proportion supplies one sufficient ground for the existential claim that *there is* a 'real number', root 2.

Yet how can we ground the analogous existential presupposition, that there is something whose square is -1? How can we justify the step from the non-existence of a *real* $\sqrt{-1}$, to the existence of an *imaginary* number, $i = \sqrt{-1}$? To address this question, I will dig back a little into the metaphysical and, to some degree, the historical soil from which imaginary numbers sprouted.

In Renaissance Italy, mathematicians used to engage in public tournaments, complete with official judges who would declare a winner. Sometimes these tournaments took the form of debates; sometimes the participants set problems for one another to solve within a specified period of time. Bets were often laid on the outcome of such tournaments; and reputations could be made or broken by the outcome. (For more, see Ore's (1953) biography of Cardano.) In such circumstances, if a mathematician could find a technique for, say, solving cubic equations, this could be of considerable value to him, even if the reasons for its success were not well understood.

Imaginary numbers thus won their way into mathematics by their utility in derivations of solutions which mathematicians could understand. Reflective mathematicians worried about the fact that they could not understand what the intermediate steps in the derivation meant; but the importance of obtaining results compelled them to tolerate this situation. The resulting tension lasted for a long time: up to Leibniz and beyond. There are some intriguing passages from Leibniz's letters to mathematicians, which throw light on the issue, collected in Gerhardt (1899) and cited in Crossley (1980). A reply to Leibniz from Huyghens nicely captures the tension:

The remark you make concerning inextractable roots, and with imaginary quantities, which however when added together yield a real quantity, is surprising and entirely novel. One would never have believed that $\sqrt{(1 + \sqrt{-3})} + \sqrt{(1 - \sqrt{-3})}$ make $\sqrt{6}$ and there is something hidden therein which is incomprehensible to me. (Cited in Crossley, 1980, p. 230.)

Let us try to see more clearly why imaginary numbers have seemed so incomprehensible, and also, how we can nevertheless find a clear meaning in them after all.

From our perspective, the problems the Renaissance mathematicians set one another seem like problems of finding *solutions to equations*: for instance,

Problem 1:
Find a real number x for which $x^2 + 10x = 39$.
(Answer: $x = 3$)

Problem 2:
Find a real number x for which $3x^3 + 18x = 60$.
(Answer: $x = 2$)

Yet viewing their problems in these bloodless, abstract, modern terms leaves out some of the flavour of their thought. The way these problems were conceived, at that time, took something more like the following form:

Problem 1:
Find a length such that, the area of a square with sides of that length, plus the area of a rectangle with one side of that length and the other side of length 10, equals 39,

Problem 2:
Find a length such that, the volume of three cubes with sides of that length, plus the area of a rectangle with one side of that length and the other side of length 18, equals 60.

This way of thinking of their problems imposed constraints on what sorts of problems had solutions which could be understood as *true* assertions about lengths, areas, and volumes.

Renaissance mathematicians were comfortable with positive real (rational or irrational) numbers. But negative numbers were of dubious intelligibility, since no line has a negative length; no polygon has negative area; and no solid has negative volume. Negative numbers began to creep in, by way of problems like:

'Find a length such that, when it is taken away from . . .'

Such problems can, they found, be deftly handled by using negative numbers; but still, they felt uneasy about what such symbolism really meant. And well they should! Fortunately, their worries about negative numbers can be laid to rest by a theory of proportions. There is no negative length, but there are negative proportions—holding, for instance, between relations like 'so much longer than' and 'so much shorter than'.

Renaissance mathematicians were comfortable enough with the *square*, x^2, and the *cube* x^3, of any positive real number x; but higher powers, x^4, x^5, . . . were of dubious intelligibility. Again, however, their doubts can be quieted by a decent theory of proportions, as was seen clearly for instance by Descartes or Newton. They argued that multiplication of two real numbers, representing say two *lengths*, *need not* be construed as yielding a measure of the *area* formed by a rectangle with sides of these lengths. Rather, multiplication of two such numbers will yield another number, which can be construed as measuring a third magnitude *of the same sort*. Thus, 'a length times a length' can be thought of as another length, rather than as an area. Being another length, it can be 'multiplied' by the given length yet again, to yield a length whose magnitude is the third power of the length we started with. There is no limit to the number of times this can be repeated. So there is no upper limit of intelligibility for higher powers of real numbers.

The foundation of multiplication lies in the theory of proportions, and is encapsulated in the following principle:

$a = b \times c$

if and only if the proportion of a to b equals the proportion of c to 1.

Stated thus briefly, the basic principle of multiplication rests on proportions holding *between numbers*, rather than between other things, as for instance, between lengths. But we can press the basis down further, so that it rests on more general principles of proportion—proportions which hold not only between numbers, but between other magnitudes too, like length.

Pick say a length for our unit; and then the real numbers a, b, c will be proportions, which various lengths have to the unit. Suppose line OA has proportion a to the unit; OB has proportion b to the unit; and OC has proportion c to the unit. Then the basic principle underlying multiplication is this:

$a = b \times c$

if and only if the proportion of OA to OB is the same as the proportion of OC to the unit length.

Given any two lines OB and OC, of lengths b and c, we can use simple geometry to construct a line OA of length $b \times c$.

From a point O draw a line OU of unit length, and continue this line (if necessary) to obtain a point C such that OC has length c (that is, so that the proportion between OC and OU is c).

From the same point O, draw a line OB, at some angle to OU, so that the length of OB is b (that is, so that the proportion between OB and OU is b).

New continue line OB (if necessary), to obtain a point A such that UB is parallel to CA (see Fig. 28). Then geometry tells us that the proportion of OA to OB is the same as the proportion of OC to the unit OU. Hence the length of OA is $a = b \times c$.

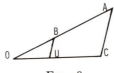

FIG. 28

When $b \times c$ is interpreted as an *area*, a kind of equivocation has been perpetrated. We can form an area of magnitude $b \times c$ in a variety of different ways. One way is by taking a unit length to form one side of a rectangle, and taking a line of length $b \times c$ to form the other side of the rectangle, as in Fig. 29. It can then be shown that the proportion between this area, and the area of a square whose side has unit length, will be the same as the proportion between the length of OA and the length of OU.

Suppose for instance that some number n of equal lengths add up to at least OU, and m of them add up to at least OA. Then just that

length $a = b \times c$

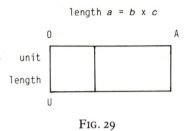

FIG. 29

number n of strips of equal area will add up to at least the unit square; and m of them will add up to at least the area of the whole rectangle. Hence, on the Whitehead–Wiener theory of proportions, whatever proportion holds between lengths OA and OU must also hold between the *areas* of the rectangle and the unit square.

The most natural way of forming a rectangle of area $b \times c$ is, of course, by taking one side to be of length b and the other of length c. That such a rectangle has area $b \times c$, however, is a fact which rests on the following facts.

Consider the areas and lines shown in Fig. 30. Suppose that O'B' and OB have the same proportion to OU, namely b; and that O'C' and OC have the same proportion to OU, namely c. Suppose also that PQRS is a 'unit square', so that each of its sides is equal to OU.

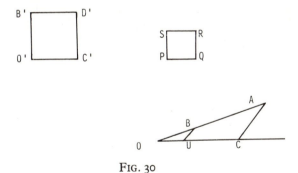

FIG. 30

Then the proportion between the *areas* of the rectangle and square are the same as the proportion of the *length* OA to OU.

This is what lies behind the Renaissance mathematician's use of real numbers to range freely over lengths, areas, and volumes. A theory of proportions renders intelligible their use of negative numbers, and of higher powers than the cube. Imaginary numbers, however, are not so easily rendered intelligible, even by the Eudoxus–Whitehead–Wiener theory of proportions.

Recall that when $a = b \times c$, then the proportion of a to b must be the same as the proportion of c to 1. Apply this to the case where $a = -1$, and $b = c = i$ say: $-1 = i \times i$.
We obtain the interpretation:

The proportion of -1 to i is the same as the proportion of i to 1.

Expanding this in the light of the theory that proportions are relations between relations, we obtain:

Definition of i:
The proportion i is that proportion *which is such that*:
if some relation R stands in proportion -1 to a relation U, and some other relation S stands in proportion i to U,
then the proportion of R to S is the same as the proportion of S to U.

We must then ask ourselves, what sorts of relations would R, S, and U have to be, in order for them to satisfy such a condition? And what sort of relation of proportion would i have to be?

On the Whitehead–Wiener theory of proportions, the idea of a proportion is, we may recall, very roughly this:

A proportion holds between relations R and S when there are relations μ for which some *specifiable pattern* of repetitions of μ will have the same outcomes as applications of R or of S.

Under this conception of proportions, it would seem that *no* proportion could possibly satisfy the conditions i is supposed to satisfy.

Consider more closely the definition of i. It requires a negative proportion, -1, to hold between R and U. This means that where you can get *to* by R you can get *from* by U (see Fig. 31). The definition of i

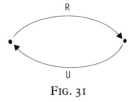

R

U

Fig. 31

also requires another relation, S, which is to stand in some proportion i to U. This further relation S must stand in some proportion to R.

Consider, in order, the two possibilities:

    (a) the proportion of R to S is positive;

    (b) the proportion of R to S is negative.

(a) Suppose that the proportion of R to S is *positive*. Then, on the Wiener theory, we will have, for specifiable relations μ, that μ^n replicates R, and μ^m replicates S (Fig. 32). Then it follows that the proportion of S to U must be negative: since m applications of μ replicates S, and n applications of the inverse of μ replicates U.

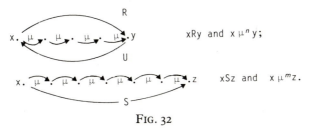

xRy and $x\,\mu^n\,y$;

xSz and $x\,\mu^m z$.

FIG. 32

Hence, if the proportion of R to S is *positive*, then the proportion of S to U is *negative*. And so the proportion of R to S cannot be the same as the proportion of S to U—as was required by the definition of i.

(b) Suppose now, instead, that the proportion of R to S is *negative*. Then, on the Wiener theory, we will have, for specifiable relations μ, that there are ways of repeating μ to replicate R, and of repeating its inverse to replicate S (Fig. 33). Then the proportion of R to S is

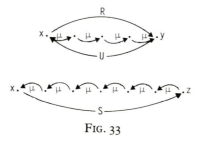

FIG. 33

negative, but the proportion of S to U must be *positive*. This is because there is a relation (the inverse of μ), such that this relation can be repeated to replicate *either* S *or* U.

And thus, the proportion of R to S, being negative, cannot be the same as the proportion of S to U, which is positive. And so again, the conditions required by the definition of i cannot be met.

What follows from this is that if S is to have the proportion i to U—if there is to be any such proportion i—then S cannot have *either* a positive *or* a negative proportion to R or U.

The relations R, S, and U must therefore be such that *no* relations μ, which can be repeated to replicate S, can also be repeated to replicate R or U.

This sets up the problem we face in trying to interpret imaginary numbers like $\sqrt{-1}$. No line, or area, or volume, or velocity, . . . can have magnitude $\sqrt{-1}$. But that is not all. No line, or area, or volume, or velocity, . . . can have magnitude -1, either; yet there can be a *proportion* of -1 holding between *relative magnitudes*. And such a notion of proportion can be explained along the lines initiated by Eudoxus. The problem we face in interpreting $\sqrt{-1}$ is especially hard, because there cannot even be a *proportion* meeting the defining characteristics of $\sqrt{-1}$. Not, at least, if we restrict the notion of proportion to the sort of relation described by Eudoxus, Whitehead, or Wiener.

14   Complex Proportions

THERE is a common conception of the development of number theory which goes something like this.

We begin with the natural numbers. We notice that we can add any two natural numbers to obtain another natural number. When we consider *subtraction*, however, we find that we cannot subtract a larger from a smaller number. We can always add, but we can't always subtract. This is untidy. Wouldn't it be neater and completer if we *could* always subtract, and obtain *an answer*, even when subtracting a larger from a smaller number? So why not just *suppose* there to be such things as negative numbers which make this possible? As long as such a supposition leads to no logical contradiction, we can explore it to our hearts' content.

We notice next, however, that although we can always *multiply* any two whole numbers, we cannot always *divide* whole numbers to yield another whole number. We find that, as we used to say at school, '2 into 7 won't go'. So to make things neater and completer, we 'extend' the number system to embrace all the *rational* numbers. Then, just as we can always multiply, so too we can always divide (except by zero).

We then find that we can make the theory of numbers still neater and completer by 'extending' it to the full class of *real* numbers. Then various sorts of patterns turn out to be much more symmetric, and various generalizations turn out to hold much more widely than formerly. For instance we will find that not only can we take an arbitrarily high *power* of any positive real number, but also we can take any arbitrary *root* of any positive real number.

Yet an asymmetry still remains. We are able to take *powers* of *negative* real numbers; and we can find *odd* roots of negative real numbers (since, for instance, -1 is the cube root of -1). Yet we cannot taken *even* roots of negative real numbers.

And so, in the interests of harmony, symmetry, elegance, generality, and so forth, we 'extend' the number system yet again, to the class of complex numbers.

This is a conception of numbers which I heartily oppose. At best, it generates a theory of 'numbers' which is a logically consistent, and no doubt an entertaining yarn, but we have been given no reason whatever to believe it to be true. Worse, it becomes difficult to understand what such a theory *means*. When, for the sake of peace and harmony, something, *i*, is posited 'whose product with itself is −1', it is difficult to understand what is *meant* by taking the 'product' of such a fictional character with itself. The whole of number theory thus becomes a meaningless game with symbols. The impression of meaningless can be intensified by assertions like the one in Fig. 34.

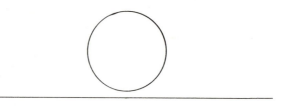

"This line meets this circle in two imaginary points"

FIG. 34

Against this I have urged that real numbers are not just posited to tidy up our symbolism. Rather, real numbers are *relations between relations*; and such relations can be discovered to be instantiated by, for instance, proportions between such magnitudes as relative lengths.

Yet what am I to make of imaginary numbers? I could, consistently, insist on a realist theory of real numbers, but nevertheless fall back on a fictionalist or formalist account of imaginary numbers. Yet I am not happy to do that. Imaginary numbers, I insist, like real numbers, are *relations between relations*. They are not just arbitrary posits, or fictional entities or illusions—a shadow-play created by a symbolism, which happens to be useful in applications even though its symbols refer to nothing real. No, imaginary numbers are genuine universals; and they are, furthermore, *instantiated* universals.

Imaginary numbers, I claim, are relations between relations. In this, they are like real numbers: that is they are somewhat like proportions, as characterized by Eudoxus, Whitehead, and Wiener.

And yet imaginary numbers cannot be *exactly* like the proportions characterized so far. In the last section, it emerged that, if *i* is to be such that $i^2 = -1$, and if *i* is to be a relation holding between relations S and U, then *there can be no suitable relations μ which can be repeated to replicate S and which can also be repeated to replicate U*.

Let me now describe some relations which display the sort of pattern required for the imaginary number i: relations which stand to one another in the proportions which constitute the imaginary numbers.

In seeking some domain which instantiates the imaginary numbers, I am aware that the most familiar and most straightforward example is geometrical, the example furnished by Argand diagrams. I will deal with this geometrical case shortly. But it is important, for my purposes, to stress that the geometrical case merely instantiates the required proportions, and does not constitute them. In this regard, imaginary numbers are like real numbers. The real numbers are instantiated in geometry, for instance, by proportions between different lengths or areas. Yet real numbers, although instantiated in geometry, are not essentially geometrical. Frege (1893–1903) says, of any numerical sign for real numbers, that:

> Certainly it denotes something, but nothing geometrical. Rather, exactly the same proportion of magnitudes which we find among line segments we should also have among durations, masses, light intensities, etc. Thereby the real number detaches itself from these specific types of magnitude and floats indiscriminately over them. And hence it seems inappropriate to let our considerations be bound too tightly to geometric images.

I entirely agree. And Frege's comments apply with equal weight to imaginary numbers, as they do to the reals.

For this reason, I will return to Quine's kinship illustration of Whitehead's theory. That illustration vividly proclaims the generality of the proportions in question. If these proportions are instantiated by the great-great-great-grandparent relation and the grandchild relation, then clearly such proportions are not in themselves geometrical, but are merely instantiated by geometrical things among others.

So I will show that Quine's kinship instantiations for the rational numbers can be extended to furnish instantiations for the imaginary numbers too.

Consider the pair of relationships:

(1) grandparenthood; great-great-great-grandparenthood.

Any two individuals who can be linked by a chain of *five* applications of the former relation, can also be linked by *two* applications of the latter relation. So there is a Whiteheadian relation of proportion holding between them: the same proportion that holds between 'two more than' ($+2$), and 'five more than' ($+5$).

Now consider instead the following pair of kinship relations:

(2) grandparenthood; cousinhood.

It is conceivable that, by repeated applications of the cousinhood relation, you might arrive at one of your ancestors who is separated from you by an even number of generations. But this is not guaranteed. It will be the exception rather than the rule.

Consequently, grandparenthood and cousinhood do not stand to each other in any straightforward Whiteheadian proportion.

And yet, I suggest, there is some sort of ratio or proportion between grandparenthood and cousinhood: there is a relationship between them which is closely analogous to a Whiteheadian proportion.

For instance, I suggest that the proportion between

(2) grandparenhood; cousinhood,

is the same as the proportion between:

(3) great-great-grandparenthood; second-cousinhood.

One pair can be converted into the other by 'doubling' or 'halving' each member of the pair.

In contrast, compare pair (2) with:

(4) grandchildhood; cousinhood.

In this case, you must take the *inverse* of the first member of one pair, in order to convert it into the other pair. So the proportion holding in case (4) differs from the proportion holding in case (2).

Now compare the pair:

(5) parenthood; cousinhood,

with the pair:

(6) cousinhood; parenthood.

One pair simply reverses the order of the other. Yet in this case, *no* combination of the taking of inverses and multiple applications will convert cousinhood into parenthood, or vice versa. So the proportion holding in (5) is importantly different from that holding in (6). And these proportions differ in a manner which is quite distinct from the manner in which (1) differs from (2), or (2) from (4).

The Whitehead method deals with proportions among relations which are, as it were, all 'aligned' with one another, in the way that for instance parenthood and grandchildhood are 'aligned'. But there should also be some way of dealing with proportions among relations which are not so 'aligned'.

The network of kinship relations is crushingly complex. So I will describe a simplified network, selected from the vast profusion of possibilities.

To simplify matters, let us suppose that intermarriage never occurs across generations. Neither Adam nor Eve coupled with their children; and similarly, neither Cain nor Abel coupled with their children, or their nephews or nieces, and so on. Thus, everyone's matrilineage, back to Eve, is of exactly the same length as their patrilineage, back to Adam.

Now imagine a culture, say Atlantis, in which *degree of relatedness* is very important, and is measured in the following way.

Firstly, note is taken of matrilineal descent. The degree of relatedness between mother and daughter, for instance, is taken to be *half* that between say the mother and her mother's mother. And so forth. This determines the fundamental sort of *diachronic* degree of relatedness in Atlantis.

Secondly, a *synchronic* degree of relatedness is defined which corresponds roughly to our characterization of cousins as first cousins, second cousins, and so forth. But there are differences. For one thing, we class together as 'cousins' both the children of our aunts and of our uncles. In Atlantis, they do not do this; rather, they classify in a manner closer to that of the ancient Romans. In Latin, there is no one word for 'cousin'. Rather, there is one word, 'patruelis' (male) or 'patruela' (female), which originally applied only to one's father's brother's child, but which came to be extended to any cousin on the father's side. And there was another word, 'consobrinus' (male) or 'consobrina' (female), which applied to any cousin on the mother's side. Notice that this relation, unlike that of cousinhood, is not symmetric; it is more like the relationship of sisterhood: if someone is my sister, this does not meant that I am their sister, since I may be their brother instead.

In Atlantis, they use something close to the Roman notion of 'consobrini', in estimating degree of synchronic relatedness. More precisely, they say that someone is their nth-sobrinus just in case their matrilineage first couples with the other person's patrilineage n generations back. And the inverse of the sobrinus relationship is called, in Atlantis, the patuelis relationship. My nth-patruelis is a person for whom I am an nth-sobrinus (see Fig. 35).

We thus have two independent ways of measuring degrees of relatedness: diachronic and synchronic. Putting these together, we

```
Marina's n-mother    :    MARRIES    :    Thalassa's n-father

              .                              .

         .                              .

    .                                        .

Marina's grandmother                Thalassa's grandfather

Marina's mother                         Thalassa's father

Marina                                        Thalassa


        Thalassa  is Marina's n-sobrinus; and

        Marina is Thalassa's n-patruelis.
```

FIG. 35

can describe a variety of other relationships analogous to the relationships we describe by such phrases as 'second cousin twice removed'.

If someone is the n-sobrinus of my m-mother, they may be called my 'n-sobrinus, m times ascended'. If someone is the n-patruelis of my m-daughter, they may be called my 'n-patruelis, m times descended'. In both cases the degree of relatedness will be $(n + m)$.

In Atlantis, everyone is taught their kinship relations. In many cultures, people are required to memorize their patrilineage; in Atlantis, they are taught to recite their relatives in ever-expanding cycles. For each degree of relatedness n, they recite the people related to them by degree n. And they do this in a conventional order. They begin with their n-mother, move through the m-sobrini of their $(n - m)$-mothers, progressing through their n-sobrini, and down to their n-daughters. Then they proceed back up the generations on their patruelis side, passing their n-patruelis, and returning to their n-mother.

Using this framework, it is possible to define the *proportions* holding between any two of the Atlantean kinship relations. To begin with, any kinship relation corresponds to the same *degree of relatedness* as some straightforward relationship of matrilineal descent. Furthermore, every kinship relation occurs a certain number of steps away from its corresponding matrilineal relationship, in the conventional order of recitation in Atlantis. So for any two kinship relations, we can determine how many steps they are from the matrilineal line. And once we have related them to the matrilineal line, we can compare them by the Whitehead method.

Suppose one kinship relation is two recitation-steps from the matrilineal line; and it corresponds to the grandmother relation on that line. Suppose another kinship relation is three recitation-steps from the matrilineal line; and it corresponds to the great-great-great-grandmother relation on that line. Then two distinct ratios are operating here. We already know from Quine that the two relationships along the matrilineal line stand in the ratio of *two to five*. And the recitation-steps separating the two kinship relations from the matrilineal line stand in the ratio of *two to three*. We can thus characterize the proportion between two Atlantean kinship relations by appeal to a *pair* of ratios.

The proportions among Atlantean kinship relations constitute, I claim, the collection of all the complex numbers $(a + ib)$, where a and b are natural numbers. The imaginary number i is not imaginary at all; it is the relationship of proportion which holds between any Atlantean kinship relation, and the kinship relationship which follows it after *one-quarter* of the recitation-steps of that degree.

More specifically, the complex numbers will be generated by systematically comparing each Atlantean kinship relation with a designated 'unit', preferably that between a child and its mother. Matrilineal relationships will then be multiples of the unit, or its inverse. Sobrinic relationships will stand in the proportion i to multiples of the unit or its inverse. And all other relationships will be combinations of these.

Thus, any two individuals linked by an Atlantean kinship relation can also be linked by two kinship relations, the first of which is a simple multiple of the unit or its inverse, and the second of which is a multiple of the unit or its inverse, 'rotated' through one-quarter of a complete recitation at that degree. And that is why the proportions between Atlantean kinship relations and the unit can all be identified with complex numbers of the form $(a + ib)$.

To further explain the nature of these proportions, I will shift away from kinship illustrations to the more traditional, spatial illustration. Note, however, that the complex numbers are here construed as relations of proportion—and these *very same* relations of proportion hold both between spatial relations and between kinship relations. Spatial relations *exemplify* the complex numbers, but complex numbers are not themselves spatial. They are exemplified by non-spatial relations as well, and Atlantean kinship relations furnish one example of such non-spatial relations instantiating the complex numbers. Nevertheless, spatial relations do furnish the pre-eminent exemplars of the complex numbers. So I turn now to geometry.

Consider a flat Euclidean two-dimensional space, with four designated directions: north, south, east, west. Consider then the relationship R which holds between any two points x and y just when y is some specific distance due east of x. Compare this with the relationship, S, which holds between two given points x and z just when z is twice that distance north-east of x (see Fig. 36).

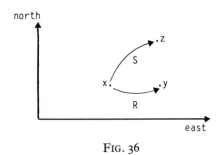

FIG. 36

The Whitehead scheme for making sense of proportions will not be applicable to these relations R and S. There is no pattern of repetitions of R which will take you to a destination that you could also reach by repetition of S.

Similarly, the Wiener scheme will not make sense of any proportions holding between R and S; there will not be any suitable relations μ which can replicate R or S by suitable patterns of repetitions.

And yet, even though no Whitehead proportion holds between R and S, it is clear that there are important relationships between R and S. And some of these relationships are closely analogous to the proportions described by Whitehead.

To elicit the relations between such relations as R and S, the key trick we need to turn is to use, not just repetitions of a *single* 'common measure', μ, but rather, to use repetitions of a combination of *two sorts* of relation. In particular, we can characterize the relationship between R and S by using a combination of a *distance* relation and a *rotation* relation.

R holds between x and y when y is some specified distance due east of x. Compare R with a relation R', which holds between x and y' when y' is twice as far due east of x (see Fig. 37). The proportion between R and R' can then be described by the usual Whitehead or Wiener method.

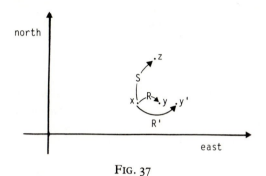

FIG. 37

Now consider the relation between R' and S. This relationship can be characterized in terms of *rotation*. The destination S takes us to is an eighth of a full rotation anticlockwise from the destination R' takes us to, and is no closer or further away.

Compare the relationship between R and S, with the relationship between two other relations, say P and Q, of the following sort. Suppose P holds between u and v just when v is some specified distance due north of u (it need not be the same distance as we had for the relation R). And Q holds between u and w just when w is $\sqrt{2}$ times that distance north-west of u, as shown in Fig. 38. In these

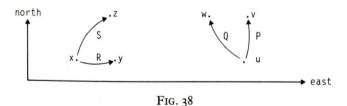

FIG. 38

circumstances, I claim, *there is* a relationship which holds both between R and S, and between P and Q. Furthermore, this relationship is *a kind* of proportion. Just as we can 'transform' R into S by a '$\sqrt{2}$-stretch' plus an '1/8-turn-anticlockwise', so too we can 'transform' P into Q by just those same operations. Or, conversely, we can transform S into R, or Q into P, by the converses of just that pair of 'stretch' and 'turn' relations.

So I claim that *the proportion between Q and P is the same as the proportion between S and R*.

Designate R as our 'unit'; and then we find that Q meets the defining characteristics for a *product* of P and S. The relation Q stands in P just as S stands to the unit; compare this with:

$$q = p \times s$$

if and only if the proportion of q to p is the same as that of s to 1.

It is no accident that the relation Q constructed by this method is precisely what is known as the *vector product* of S and P.

There is a special case worth singling out: that in which S is the same relation as P. Then Q will be the product of S with S—the square of S.

To specialize further, let R remain the same relation as before, the relation taking you some specified (unit) distance due eastwards. But change S to the relation which takes you just that same (unit) distance due north. Then Q will be the 'square' of S just when the proportion between Q and S is the same as the proportion between S and R. And that will be so just when Q takes you just as far due west as R took you due east: this is shown in Fig. 39. The proportion between Q and S is the same as that between S and R, because in each case we can transform one relation into the other by a zero-stretch plus a quarter-turn rotation clockwise.

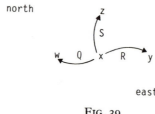

FIG. 39

If we designate relation R as our unit, then the proportion between Q and S is the same as that between S and 1. If we look back to the definition of i we find that *the proportion of S to R* meets *precisely* the requirements which are set on the imaginary number $i = \sqrt{-1}$. And so, I propose: the square root of -1 *is* the *proportion* which holds between S and R.

This yields a theory of imaginary numbers which echoes the

traditional, so-called geometrical interpretation of imaginary numbers. There is, however, a respect in which I wish to distance my theory from specifically geometrical considerations. I claim that imaginary numbers are proportions which are instantiated by geometrical relations. They are proportions which *do hold* between such relations as 'so far in this direction from' and 'thus far in that direction from'. And yet, I wish to add, there may also be quite different, wholly non-geometrical relations, which also instantiate those very same relations of proportion.

This can be made clearer by recalling the way in which Whitehead or Wiener's theory of proportions applies in relations generally, and not just to spatial relations in particular. Suppose, then, we have two relations R and S which are *not* linked in the way required by Whitehead's theory of proportions. But suppose that there is one Whitehead-proportion between R and some intermediate relation R' and then another Whitehead-proportion between R' and S. Under such circumstances—roughly—*there will be* a proportion of the 'imaginary' sort between R and S. There is no need for R or S to be a geometrical relation as long as the required two-step Whitehead-style linkages hold between R and S.

The most famous non-geometrical interpretation of imaginary numbers, due to Gauss, is by way of *ordered pairs* of real numbers. The proportion between two pairs of real numbers

$$\langle a,b \rangle \text{ and } \langle c,d \rangle$$

is defined to be the same as that between

$$\left\langle \frac{(ac + bd)}{(c^2 + d^2)} , \frac{(bc - ad)}{(c^2 + d^2)} \right\rangle \text{ and } \langle 1,0 \rangle.$$

It then follows that the proportion between $\langle -1,0 \rangle$ and $\langle 0,1 \rangle$ is the same as that between $\langle 0,1 \rangle$ and $\langle 1,0 \rangle$. And this ensures that the proportion between $\langle 0,1 \rangle$ and $\langle 1,0 \rangle$ satisfies the requirements for being the imaginary number i, provided we designate $\langle 1,0 \rangle$ as our unit.

On my account, imaginary numbers are 'two-stage proportions', which can be instantiated both geometrically and arithmetically. The geometrical instantiations are, in some respects, more illuminating. The existence of those geometrical instantiations makes it intelligible why imaginary numbers are so useful in such applications as electromagnetic theory, where electric and magnetic fields oscillate perpendicularly to one another, and can be both 'stretched' and 'rotated'. This is why i appears in many equations dealing with things like the polarization of light, or with electronics and circuitry.

Yet the purely arithmetical instantiation of imaginary proportions, by way of ordered pairs, has an appeal of its own. It enables the pure mathematician to steer clear of any dubious, contingent assumptions about space. Imaginary numbers, like real numbers, are proportions which are most *strikingly* instantiated by spatial relations. And yet, by choosing purely arithmetical instantiations instead, we can minimize our reliance on things which lie outside mathematics itself. Mathematics, on its own, can supply us with number-pairs which instantiate imaginary proportions, without need of any appeal to anything else.

Similar comments can apply to the case of real numbers, too. Their most *striking* instantiations are spatial ones. And yet, as with imaginary numbers, purely arithmetical instantiations can also be given by using *sets* constructed from natural numbers. Again, the advantage derived from focusing on non-geometrical instantiations is that this increases the autonomy of pure mathematics from physics.

The search for a non-geometrical grounding, first for imaginary, and then for real numbers, has been the primary motive which led to the birth of set theory. Natural numbers, by themselves, were not enough to furnish instantiations for the real and imaginary numbers; they had to be forged into ordered pairs, and sets of ordered pairs, and sets of sets of ordered pairs.

And once sets themselves had begun interbreeding, it became unnecessary to use sets of *numbers* to instantiate natural, real, or imaginary numbers. All the numbers you ever wanted (natural, real, or imaginary)—and more besides—could be instantiated by *pure sets*. A set is a pure set if it contains no members which are not pure sets. Thus for instance, the empty set Φ is (vacuously) pure. And so the set $\{\Phi\}$ is also pure. And so is $\{\Phi, \{\Phi\}\}$. And so on.

By instantiating all numbers by pure sets, we ensure a very high degree of autonomy for pure mathematics. We minimize the risk that upheavals in physics, or some other realm, will have any repercussions for the theory of numbers. And, it was hoped, we could thereby ensure that the theory of numbers remains a body of *necessary truths*, knowable a priori.

II(d) SETS

15 From Universals to Sets

THE relationship between *sets* and the theory of *universals* is far from clear. It is important for me to come to terms with this issue if I am to maintain the thesis that mathematics is the theory of universals. Mathematics has become difficult to distinguish from set theory. And so it would be nice, for me, if sets were universals. I am not quite forced to say that sets are universals. I could say sets are abstract individuals, which are of particular importance in mathematics because they instantiate all the universals which mathematics studies. But such a treatment of sets, as abstract individuals, underplays the closeness of fit between set theory and the theory of universals.

Naïve set theory was the result of assuming the so-called *comprehension axiom*, that *whenever there is somehow that certain things are, then there is something—a one over many—to which these things are somehow related*.

From,

> There is somehow that these things are.
> ∃ Φ.(Φ*a* & Φ*b* & . . .)

the comprehension axiom infers,

> There is something such that, there is somehow that these things are related to it.
> ∃ *x* ∃ ε.(*a*ε*x* & *b*ε*x* & . . .).

Yet the comprehension axiom is mistaken; it is a mistake to think such an inference can always be drawn. However, set theory is based on the less sweeping claim that in a specifiable, broad category of cases, even though not in all, the inference from 'somehow' to 'something' does lead from a truth to a truth.

Consider then the theory that for every open sentence of some specifiable, broad range, there is something corresponding to that open sentence, and everything which the open sentence is *true of* will be related in some important way to that something.

Such a theory is, so far, neutral between a theory of universals and a theory of sets. It is neutral about whether what corresponds to an open sentence is a set, and the things the open sentence is true of are members of that set; or whether what corresponds to the open sentence is a universal, and the things instantiate that universal.

The crucial watershed between set theory and the theory of universals comes with what is known as the principle of *extensionality*. Sets meet a principle of extensionality: that is to say *there are no distinct sets with all their members in common*. Yet two universals may be distinct, even if they do have the same intances. So a theory about 'sets and their members' is not the same thing as a theory about 'universals and their instances'. Or so it would seem.

We could, however, consider taking a bold stand—as Quine (1953) seems to do, for instance in chapter 6 of *From a Logical Point of View*—and claim that universals *are* sets, appearances not withstanding. We are confronted with two theories, one with a principle of extensionality, and one without. Regard these as two *rival* theories about universals. Set theory is then a theory which claims, against tradition, that for any two distinct universals, there will always be something which instantiates one but not the other.

This bold Quinean stand is unsatisfying; let me try to explain why. Suppose there are two distinct universals and that, in conformity with the principle of extensionality, there are indeed some things which instantiate one but not the other. For simplicity, suppose there is just one thing which instantiates one but not the other. Then ask the question: What if that thing had not existed? We would like to be able to say that, *even if* that thing had not existed, other things would still have had the same two distinct properties. So it should be at least *possible* that there should be a violation of extensionality.

Thus, I argue, there is at least this difference between universals and sets: that it is possible for there to be distinct universals with the same instances, whereas it is not possible for there to be distinct sets with the same members.

Quine could stand his ground. He could maintain that it is not possible for there to be two distinct universals with the same instances. Or, better, he could regard the whole question, of whether or not such a thing is possible, as too blunt to cut any ice.

Yet such a stubborn stand yields a theory so far removed from the traditional theory of universals that it serves no useful purpose to insist that it is still a theory of universals. Quine has deeply held reasons for believing that there is no truth of the matter, whether it is or is not still a theory of universals. And yet, all the same, it would be less confusing if we described such a theory as one which speaks of sets *rather than* universals.

Hence, on balance, it is inadvisable to identify a universal with the set of its instances.

The conclusion, however, is only that a universal is not the set of its *actual* instances. None of the considerations advanced so far will count against the proposal that a universal is the set of all its actual *and possible* instances.

Such a theory can take several forms: here is one paradigm form it could take. We could construe a universal as a class of ordered pairs of the form $\langle w, a \rangle$, where w is a possible world and a is an individual. Then, to say that 'a certain *universal* is instantiated by a in world w', is to be interpreted as equivalent to saying that a certain *class* (which is really the same thing as the universal) contains the ordered pair $\langle w, a \rangle$ as a member.

I have been quite head over heels with enthusiasm for 'possible worlds' theories of this sort, especially in semantics. I still am. Yet I am reluctant to wheel them in here. One reason springs from a long-term project I want to keep open. I hope that an adequate theory of universals should give an explanation of the grounds for *necessity* and *possibility*. Possible worlds may perhaps be identified with uninstantiated universals of some sort, or with constructions, built using universals as raw materials. Once possible worlds have been constructed, we can then use them to construct such things as 'classes of world-thing pairs' too. But universals cannot actually *be* such classes if they are (as I hope) constituents involved in their construction.

In any case, the construction of universals, using sets and possibilia, is beside the point from the perspective I am taking here. Sets emerged in mathematics; and I claim that mathematics is the theory of universals. So I am searching for ways in which the theory of universals could have *generated* set theory. A theory which constructs universals from sets completely reverses the direction of explanation that I am seeking. It shows how set theory, plus possibilia, can generate a theory of (facsimiles of) universals. But it leaves it mysterious where sets come from. And that is what I want to find out.

How then could the theory of universals have generated set theory? Here is one possible way. Suppose we begin with a generous platonic theory, postulating *at least one* universal for *almost* every open sentence. We may then notice a specific relation among universals—the relation of coextensiveness. This relation will be an equivalence relation; it will be reflexive, symmetric, and transitive. Suppose we symbolize it thus: when a universal x is coextensive with a universal y, we write '$x = y$'. Our theory of universals, expressed like that, will look just like set theory.

Perhaps that is how we should interpret set theory. Perhaps set theory is really a partial theory of universals, one which abstracts from all facts which hinge on whatever distinctions there may or may not be among coextensive universals. Describing it slightly differently, we might say that a *set* is what a collection of coextensive universals all have in common. Or, more playfully, a class is an equivalence class of universals.

This explains one possible route from a theory of universals to set theory. It presupposes, however, that there is *at least one* universal for each set. And it would be nice to be given an explanation of what *sort* of universal could reasonably be expected to correspond to any given arbitrary, heterogeneous, gerrymandered, random set which mathematics might call for. Just what *do* all members of a random set have in common? Indeed, if they did have something in common, would the set really be random? To give a satisfying ground for set theory within the theory of universals, I need to say something more about what universals there are, and why we should suppose there to be at least one for each set.

16 Sets and Essences

Why should we assume at least one universal for every set? One source for such an assumption lies in the assumption that for every truth, there must be things in the world which make it true. And this draws us towards the doctrine that there must be something, a universal, corresponding to each open sentence which can be used in true predications. Just as there is a set for every open sentence which can be used in true predications, so too there must be a universal, a truthmaker, for each such true predication.

I will examine the notion of truthmakers, and their relationship to sets and universals, in the latter part of this book. For the moment, however, I will explore a different route to the doctrine that there is a universal for every set.

Consider any finite number of things, $a_1, a_2, \ldots, a_n$. It has been remarked, for instance by Hilbert and Bernays (1971), and by Gödel (1944), that there will always be an open sentence which is true of all and only these things, namely the open sentence:

$(x = a_1)$ or $(x = a_2)$ or . . . or $(x = a_n)$.

Now imagine that there is a universal corresponding to each such open sentence. And suppose there are such universals for infinite pluralities, as well as finite ones. We are then well on the way towards identifying sets with universals. We might conjecture: a set is just a disjunctive universal of precisely this sort—a set *is* just the property of 'being a_1, or being a_2, or . . .'.

This theory need rest only on the conjecture that, for each thing a, there is the property of *being a*:

$(x = a)$,

together with the conjecture that for any plurality of properties, there *is* a *disjunctive* property, which is possessed by anything that has any one of those properties.

There are, however, reasons for being dissatisfied with this theory of sets as disjunctive universals. Here is one reason. Suppose we are dealing with spatially located things a_1, a_2, and so on. And suppose we grant that there is a property common to all and only these things. A property, however, may be appropriately described as located wherever any thing is which instantiates it. So a property common to

a_1, a_2, and so on will be located where a_1 is, and located where a_2 is, and so on. Yet the *set* of these things is *not* located where a_1 is, *nor* where a_2 is, and so on. So the set is not a common property of these things.

Notice, however, that this argument threatens specifically the doctrine that a set is a *property*. It would have no force against the doctrine that a set is a *relation*. Suppose we were to suggest that the set containing a_1, a_2, and so on, is a relation holding among these things a_1, a_2, and so on. Where could such a relation be located? In common with all relations, we need locate it no more precisely than by saying: this relation exists *within any region which contains all the related things*. But this creates no tension between such a relation and a set. It is equally natural to say that a *set* exists within any region which contains all its members.

So far then we have a reason for being suspicious of the theory that a set is a disjunctive property. But we should keep in mind that this reason does not weigh against an alternative theory of sets as relations of some sort.

There is another reason for dissatisfaction with the theory of sets as disjunctive properties. We may ask: Why should we believe there is some *single* property corresponding to the open sentence

$$(x = a_1) \text{ or } (x = a_2) \text{ or } \ldots \text{ or } (x = a_n)?$$

This open sentence is true of a_1: but why? Because $a_1 = a_1$. It has the property of 'being a_1, or a_2, or $\ldots$' *because it has the property of being* a_1. In contrast, consider why this open sentence is true of a_2. Why? a_2 has the property of 'being a_1, or a_2, or $\ldots$' *because it has the property of being* a_2.

Thus a_1 has the property of *being* a_1; a_2 has the property of *being* a_2. These are two distinct properties. The same open sentence is true of both a_1, and a_2; but it is true of each in virtue of a different property. There is no need for any single, 'disjunctive' property shared by both.

For these reasons I urge that we return to the idea I shelved earlier: the idea that a set might be a *relation* rather than a property.

Consider an open sentence with n free variables, $x_1 \, x_2, \ldots, x_n$:

$$(x_1 = a_1) \,\&\, (x_2 = a_2) \,\&\, \ldots \,\&\, (x_n = a_n).$$

An open sentence with n free variables will correspond to an *n-place relation* if it corresponds to any universal at all.

I conjecture that there is such a relation. It is a relation which holds among the members of the set a_1, a_2, $\ldots$, a_n, and among no other things. It is located in exactly those regions which contain that whole set. And the dubiousness of a disjunctive property no longer applies, since this relation is built out of conjunction instead of disjunction.

The relation I am describing is the relation which holds among some things if and only if these things *are* a_1, a_2, and so on. The open sentence

$$(x_1 = a_1) \ \& \ (x_2 = a_2) \ \& \ldots \& \ (x_n = a_n)$$

may be read as:

'. . . are the things $a_1, a_2, \ldots, a_n$'.

This relation is a plural version of properties of the form 'being a'—properties coresponding to predicates of the form

$$(x = a).$$

Some have held that the property of 'being a' is primitive, simple, and unanalysable. Conceived thus, it has been called a *haecceity* (a medieval latin term meaning 'thisness'). The property of 'being a', it is argued, cannot be analysed in qualitative terms, as any combination of features which a could share with other things. The reason given is that for any such combination of shareable features, it is possible that there should be two numerically distinct *duplicates*, a and b, which share all those qualitative features without being identical. Such duplicates, being non-identical, cannot have the same thisnesses: a has the property of being a, whereas b has the property of being b. Hence these two distinct properties, being a, and being b, cannot be identified with qualitative features, all of which a and b share.

On such a theory of haecceities, my account of sets becomes this: *a set is a plural haecceity*. A set is the *theseness* of its members.

Yet I do not need to be saddled with a doctrine of haecceities simply by my account of sets as relations. Perhaps the argument from duplicates can be blocked. Perhaps the property of 'being a' can be qualitatively analysed after all. That is to say it could be argued that for each individual a, there will be a conjunction of properties which are individually necessary and jointly sufficient for a thing to be a—a could not exist without those properties: *only a could have *all* these properties, and necessarily anything with all those properties would be a. This conjunction of properties can be called the *individual essence* for a. And the property of 'being a' could then be identified with just this conjunctive property.

On this analysis of the property of 'being a', my account of sets becomes this: a set is a plural essence.

This phrase, 'plural essence', may perhaps be pressed into duty for both haecceitist and non-haecceitist theories. Both theories, we may say, describe a set as a plural essence. What distinguishes the haecceitists is their claim that an individual essence, and hence a plural essence, is unanalysable in qualitative terms.

I claim that this conception of a set as a plural essence is consonant with the mathematiclly central conception of sets, as captured for instance in the now orthodox, Zermelo–Fraenkel set theory (ZF).

Set theory initially led to contradictions, the simplest of which was Russell's paradox. But this was due to an infection contracted from Truthmaker, the notion that every truth requires a 'truthmaker', a notion to be examined in Part III. This 'infected' conception of sets has been called, for instance by Gödel (1944), *the intensional conception of sets*. But there is also an alternative conception of sets—one which, as Gödel says, has given rise to no known antinomies. This alternative has been called *the iterative conception of sets*, or the conception of sets as a *cumulative hierarchy*.

There is a certain sort of imagery which goes along with the so-called iterative conception of sets. Imagine we begin with a domain of individuals which are not sets. We then 'apply' the set-membership relation to these, thereby 'generating' a profusion of sets of individuals. These sets are harvested, and are then planted back down in the domain among the individual non-sets we started with. The set-membership relation is then 'applied' over again, exactly as it was the first time. This time the set-membership relation will 'generate' sets whose members are either non-sets, or sets of non-sets. This new harvest of sets is again added to the domain, and the procedure is repeated. Imagine that each planting and harvest takes half as long as the one before. Then if this procedure is repeated over and over, in a finite amount of time we will have reaped an infinite harvest, just as an arrow, in flying across a room, passes through an infinite sequence of shorter and shorter distances, in a finite time. Having thus reaped an infinite harvest of sets, we can begin again: treating this total harvest as our domain, 'applying' the set-membership relation, and reaping new harvests as before. There is no limit to the number of times this sequence of operations could be performed.

Boolos (1971) and Wang (1974) have explained at some length how a conception of this sort gives rise to the axioms of Zermelo–Fraenkel set theory, the standard system among working mathematicians. And, most importantly, it seems to supply enough sets to instantiate all the relations of *proportion*, the real numbers, which grew out of the study of space and motion.

The metaphor of growth, which accompanies the iterative conception of sets, is unsatisfying. The theory that sets are plural essences can go some way towards transferring insubstantial metaphor into substantial metaphysics. Given a domain of non-sets, *there will be* their plural essence. This then is a further existent; this plural essence will be a thing which 'is what it is and not another thing'. This plural essence, *e* say, will have the property of 'being an *x* such that $(x = e)$'; and nothing else will have this property. And this *individual* essence will be conjoinable with other such generating *plural* essences—of 'being *these* things: . . .'. Plural essences will thus form a cumulative hierarchy of just the sort which ZF set theory describes.

There are sceptics who would rather not believe in sets. I have given a description of what it is that they are sceptical about. They are sceptical about whether there are any such things as sets; sets are plural essences; so their scepticism is warranted if there really are no such things as plural essences. And it is not hard to sympathize with such scepticism. Is there really any such thing as the property of 'being *a*'?

I am doubtful whether there is any real distinction between the property of 'being *a*', and the thing *a* itself. Yet the issues are still very murky. If, in the end, we decide there are no plural essences, then my theory would commit me to saying there are no such things as sets. But how serious a threat would this pose for a realist theory of mathematics such as I am backing? If I were to take an anti-realist stand on sets, I would conclude that the universals studied in mathematics—numbers for instance—are not after all instantiated *by sets*. It does not follow, however, that they are not instantiated by anything. They may still be instantiated, for instance by space. So anti-realism over sets would not force me to anti-realism over mathematics. The worst that need follow is that mathematics is less pure and autonomous than pure mathematicians have hoped.

17   Sets and Consistency

NATURAL numbers are many-place relations of mutual distinctness. Real and imaginary numbers are relations between relations. This is what I have argued.

An important source of uneasiness about mathematics concerns the apparent *necessity* of mathematics, as contrasted with the *contingency* of facts about whether various middle-sized dry-goods instantiate various universals. Suppose, for instance, that there are only finitely many individuals in the world. Then it would seem that, on my theory, very large numbers would be uninstantiated. Or suppose that space is not as it seems to be, suppose for instance that it is not continuous, and so does not satisfy the presuppositions which underly the claim that there are irrational proportions, like $\sqrt{2}$. If space were not as I suppose it to be, then perhaps some real and imaginary numbers would be uninstantiated, at least by space.

Let me grant for the moment that my theory might land in trouble if there *were* only finitely many things, or if space *were* dicontinuous, and so forth. But why should I worry about these possibilities? There *are* infinitely many things, and space *is* continuous. Someone asks me to imagine what would happen to my theory if things were otherwise. But why should I not reply: 'I might be in trouble if these things *were* so; but they aren't, so I'm not!'?

There is, however, a kind of uneasiness which is not dissipated by the mere confidence that the universals in question all do happen to be instantiated. Even if there are infinitely many things, and even if space is continuous, the feeling remains that this is only a contingent fact—it could have been false. Furthermore, it would seem that this is an *empirical* fact which cannot be known without relying, directly or indirectly, on experience of the contingent world. And these contingent and empirical elements in my theory would seem to obstruct any attempt I might make to explain the non-contingent and a priori aura surrounding mathematics.

There is a range of responses I could explore here. I could try biting the bullet—admitting that my theory commits me to a characterization of mathematics as contingent and empirical—and simply standing by that commitment. I could refer to Quine (1953) as an able recent defender of related doctrines, notably in 'Two Dogmas of

Empiricism'. This hard-line stand is not really to my liking. But I will not try to show what is wrong with it: I will counter it only by exploring alternatives.

There is another response I could try out, by way of drawing on a point of contention traditionally associated with the opposing theories of Plato and Aristotle concerning universals. An *Aristotelian* theory is generally taken to be one which requires that a universal must be instantiated if it is to exist: that *there are no* universals which nothing has. The opposing view, that there are universals which have no instances, can appropriately be called a Platonist theory, in one of the senses of that slippery label.

A Platonist then could agree that it is contingent which numbers are instantiated, but maintain that their existence, and their interrelations, are non-contingent and knowable a priori. These universals *would* exist and be interrelated in the ways they are, even if they *were* uninstantiated.

However, as I read it, the general flow of pure mathematics in recent history has not been towards the sort of Platonist theory. Rather, the tendency has been one of postulating a profusion of *necessarily instantiated* universals. If spatial things do not necessarily instantiate all the numbers, then there must be some *other* things which do, namely sets.

There are thus two rival theories, which may be called 'instantiated Platonism' and 'uninstantiated Platonism'. According to the former, universals exist because they are necessarily instantiated; according to the latter, they all exist even though some of them are or could be uninstantiated. Mathematics, I claim, has mostly opted for instantiated Platonism.

One advantage which is sometimes cited for instantiated Platonism, is that one very good way of being assured that a theory is *consistent* is by finding things which actually have all the properties and relations which the theory postulates. Many mathematicians assume that consistency is *all* they need to establish: Hilbert for instance. Yet consistency cannot be established *ex nihilo*. As Frege stressed in his letters to Hilbert the best assurance that a theory is consistent is by finding an interpretation which makes the theory *true* (see Kluge, 1971). If we look closely at Hilbert's programme, in fact, we find that he does at least rely on the literal truth of a fragment of mathematics, as applied to properties and relations of the *symbols* mathematicians use.

So there is at least one advantage which instantiated Platonism has over its uninstantiated rival: that of providing an assurance of consistency.

But there is another reason why instantiated Platonism is more interesting than its rival. Suppose we were to imagine that numbers exist which seem to be uninstantiated. Then we would be able to count them. And we could thereby show that these very numbers *instantiate one another*. So it would follow that they were not uninstantiated after all, as we had imagined. So if there were for instance *any* two things—two spatial things perhaps, or two sets, or even the numbers zero and one—then the number two will be instantiated. And so there will be three things altogether—the first two together with the number two itself. Thus the number three is instantiated too. And so on.

Similarly, if real numbers were imagined to exist, even though they seemed to be uninstantiated, then we would find that they stand in various relationships of proportion *to one another*. Even if the proportion $\sqrt{2}$ did not hold between the diagonal and side of any square, that proportion would still hold between the real numbers $\sqrt{2}$ and 1, between 2 and $\sqrt{2}$, and so forth. So, since real numbers are in fact relations of proportion, it follows that if there were real numbers, then they would *instantiate one another*. Hence they could not have been uninstantiated after all, as we had imagined. We cannot suppose real numbers to exist uninstantiated, since if they exist at all, they must be instantiated—at least by one another.

And so, let us set aside uninstantiated Platonism in favour of instantiated Platonism. If numbers exist at all, they are instantiated.

But do numbers exist at all? If one were nervous about the very existence of numbers, it would be little consolation to be told that they are instantiated—by one another! So it does seem important to find some assurance, outside the numbers themselves, that there are indeed things which instantiate the numbers.

In the case of natural numbers, it is pretty obvious that at least the smaller numbers are instantiated. If you are obsessed by a desire for meticulous hygiene in pure mathematics, then you can perhaps draw on set theory to provide us with sufficiently 'pure' instantiations for even the smallest natural numbers. And yet if that is all we needed sets for, this would provide a pretty tenuous motive for set theory.

There is, however, a much more powerful motive for introducing set theory. Sets provide instantiations, not only for the natural numbers, but also for the real numbers. And in the case of real numbers, it is much more important to establish clear instantiations—not only to establish the consistency of the theory, but also to map out clearly just what truths do hold for real numbers, and why.

If we had not been shaken by the triumph of Einstein's non-Euclidean theory of physical space, then we might have been less diffident than we are about calling upon physical space to instantiate all the real numbers. It does *seem* obvious that space has the properties required by the theory of real numbers. It does seem obvious, for instance, that there are square regions of space with half the area of other square regions. It does seem obvious that when two lines 'cross', there must be some point which they share in common. And so forth. Given enough truths of this sort, it follows that spatial relations will instantiate all the proportions I identify with the real numbers.

And yet there has been no shortage of sceptics who, like Hume (see Selby-Bigge, 1960), argue that what seems obvious to mathematicians need not be true. And of course, since Einstein, we have still more reason for such scepticism. Current theories of physical space do still treat it as continuous, and as instantiating all the real numbers. But what physics tells us is *true* of space seems in many respects to be quite the obverse of obvious. And even the continuity of space has sometimes seemed threatened by developments in quantum mechanics.

The problems over physical space are worse, however, than just worries about whether certain truths are obvious. There are worries about *which* truths hold for space. In the analysis of rates of change of magnitudes like velocity, patterns of reasoning became indispensable, even though they occasionally led to contradictions. Contradictions were apt to emerge whenever *infinity* entered the picture.

Galileo described some of the more strikingly mystifying features of infinities (see Crew and de Salvio, 1954, pp. 31–2). He noted, for instance, that there is one-to-one correlation of each natural number with a perfect square, a number which, like 16, or 25, or 36, is the square of a natural number. When there is such a one-to-one correlation between one plurality and another it is natural to infer that these pluralities have the same number. And yet the perfect squares are only *some* of the numbers taken all together; so it is natural to infer that there are fewer perfect squares than there are natural numbers. Galileo concluded that number should not be applied to infinite pluralities: that we cannot consistently speak of 'more', or 'fewer', or 'as many', when speaking of infinities.

But there is another puzzle case Galileo noted (see Crew and de Salvio, 1954, pp. 20–5 and 49–52), which serves extremely well as an illustration of just *how* mystifying the continuity of space really is.

Imagine two concentric circles drawn on a rigid wheel: call the larger one the *rim*, the smaller one the *hub*, and their common centre the *axis*. Imagine that the wheel rolls on its rim, without slipping, for one complete turn. Then its bottom point will trace out a line, RR' say, which is as long as the circumference of the rim.

Now imagine a line, HH' say, which stretches from the bottom point of the hub at the starting position to its bottom point at the finishing position as shown in Fig. 40.

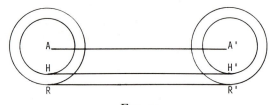

FIG. 40

Since the wheel is rigid, and the three points A, H, R are collinear at the starting position, they will still be collinear at the finishing position.

Now consider the manner in which the inner circle, the hub, rolls along the line HH'. There will be no 'slipping': that is no point on the hub will slide through several points on HH'. Rather, each point on the hub will touch one and only one point on HH'. Similarly, there will be no 'skipping': that is no point on the line HH' will fail to be touched by the hub as it rolls past. Rather, each point on HH' will be touched by one and only one point on the hub.

The manner in which the hub rolls along HH' is thus exactly like the manner in which the rim rolls along RR'. We inferred from the manner the rim rolled along RR' that the line RR' has the same length as the circumference of the rim. So by parity of reasoning, we should infer that HH' has the same length as the circumference of the hub. Yet this is absurd.

Galileo's puzzles can be resolved. But they do raise deep questions about just what truths *do* hold for space and spatial relations. And notice that the currently accepted resolutions of Galileo's puzzles, descending from Cantor (1895), draw heavily upon the resources of set theory. The great achievement of set theory has been that it provides a very good way of sorting out exactly what truths do and do not hold for real numbers.

I will give one other illustration of the sources of uneasiness over the continuity of space. This illustration comes from one of the great architects of contemporary mathematics, Henri Lebesgue (1966, p. 98), who revolutionized the foundations of integration and measure theory. (See Fig. 41 for the geometrical figure described in the following passage).

Formerly, when I was a schoolboy, the teachers and pupils had been satisfied with this reasoning by passage to the limit. However, it ceased to satisfy me when some of my schoolmates showed me, along about my fifteenth year, that one side of a triangle is equal to the sum of the other two and that $\pi = 2$. Suppose that ABC is an equilateral triangle and that D, E, and F are the midpoints of BA, BC, and CA. The length of the broken line BDEFC is AB + AC. If we repeat this procedure with the triangles DBE and FEC, we get a broken line of the same length made up of eight segments, etc. Now these broken lines have BC as their limit, and hence the limit of their lengths, that is, their common length AB + AC, is equal to BC. The reasoning with regard to π is analogous.

Nothing, absolutely nothing, distinguishes this reasoning from what we used to evaluate the circumference and area of a circle, the surface and volume of a cylinder, a cone, and a sphere. This result has been extremely instructive to me.

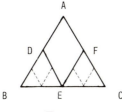

FIG. 41

It is instructive to note that the way Lebesgue resolved such puzzles drew very heavily on set theory.

For these reasons, it was important to find instantiations of the real numbers *other than* the real numbers themselves, and other than spatial relations, too. The stunning success of set theory has been that of supplying clear, and clearly understood, instantiations of the real numbers. Given the existence of sets, we can specify clearly how relations of proportion can be instantiated among sets. And this enables us to sort out clearly just what is and what is not true of them.

One of the things set theory was supposed to do was to provide non-spatial instantiations for the real numbers. And this it succeeded in doing. But it was also supposed to provide a proof of the consistency of the theory of real numbers. And it has not been quite such an unqualified success at doing that. Set theory gave birth to contradictions of its own.

However, the set-theoretical contradictions arise from semantics, from assumptions concerning what I call truthmakers. I will argue that universals, as the subject-matter of mathematics, must not be construed as truthmakers. And when sets are construed as genuine universals, and not as truthmakers, the result is the iterative conception of sets, as a cumulative hierarchy—as captured for instance in Zermelo–Fraenkel (ZF) set theory.

We have none but question-begging proofs of the consistency of such a theory as ZF. And yet its consistency is not seriously in doubt. Hence, the fact that real numbers are instantiated among sets does provide some genuine reassurance, even if not absolute proof, of the consistency of the theory of real numbers.

And yet the importance of set theory should not be overestimated. I have argued that numbers are universals—and also that sets are universals. But numbers are not themselves sets. Rather, they are universals which are instantiated by sets, amongst other things. Sets are only some among the many universals studied by mathematics.

Once we have recognized numbers as existing, we then find that numbers instantiate one another. Natural numbers *can be counted*. Real numbers *stand in proportions* to one another. And also, real numbers can be counted; and natural numbers stand in proportions.

This begins to cast some light on why mathematics has the very distinctive character it does have: why it is described as dealing with *necessary* truths (whatever that really means), and why it seems to generate truths which we can know a priori (whatever that really amounts to). Mathematics deals with patterns, structures, properties, relations . . . universals . . . which are instantiated by contingent beings, no doubt, but which also instantiate one another. And thus, even if mathematicians begin their journey among contingencies, their mathematics soon begins to lift off the contingent world, and to become autonomous and self-sustaining. It is this reflexiveness, this autonomy, which underlies the non-contingent and a priori aura surrounding pure mathematics.

OO : XX :: XX : OO

III TRUTH AND EXISTENCE

18   Functions and Arguments

MATHEMATICS, I have argued, is the theory of universals. And the universals it investigates include the numbers: natural, real, and imaginary numbers. Natural numbers are relations of n-fold mutual distinctness which hold among individuals. Real and imaginary numbers are relations of proportions which hold among relations.

This theory requires that there be such things as properties and relations, things traditionally called universals; and it requires that these things *exist* in whatever sense is required to permit them to stand as the subject-matter of investigations. This requires us to eschew nominalism and embrace some form of realism about universals.

I will not attempt to refute nominalism; nor will I say a great deal in defence of realism. What I do wish to do, however, is to say something more about the nature of universals.

My thesis is that mathematics is concerned with universals in the sense of *recurrences*; these recurrences exist in nature and we recognize them, and reflect them in our language. Yet they are not generated by language. They would still have existed even if language hadn't.

So I wish to distance myself from theories which rest their claims about universals solely or primarily on considerations about language. In order to do this, I need to explore the linguistic slant on universals in some detail.

The conclusion I reach is that, while there may very well be universals which are creatures of language, these universals are not the subject-matter of mathematics. The creatures of language, I call *truthmakers*. They are entities whose entire *raison d'être* is to explain what makes a linguistic item true. Truthmakers, I claim, are not the subject-matter for mathematics.

Recurrence universals are the subject-matter for mathematics; and they contribute to the process of truthmaking, just as individuals do. But their contribution is no different in kind from that offered by individuals. The existence of individuals alone is, in general, not enough to provide a truthmaker; nor is the existence of recurrence universals alone; nor is the existence of individuals and recurrence universals together. Truthmaking requires something more than the sorts of universals which furnish the subject-matter of mathematics.

And conversely, and very importantly, the presumed need for truthmakers cannot justify the introduction of the sorts of universals which constitute the numbers and the other mathematical entities. The source of mathematics does not lie in symbols. The symbols in mathematics represent a reality beyond themselves. Those who hanker after an a priori foundation for mathematics cannot find it in language.

The hallowed path from language to universals has been by way of the *correspondence theory of truth*: the doctrine that whenever something is true, there must be something in the world which makes it true. I will call this the Truthmaker axiom. The desire to find an adequate truthmaker for every truth has been one of the sustaining forces behind traditional theories of universals.

It has also been one of the forces behind the attempt to find secure, a priori foundations for mathematics. The assumption that for each truth there must exist an adequate truthmaker has been used to generate the existence of mathematical objects.

On the Pythagorean standpoint I have been defending, mathematics studies universals. It would be nice to find some guarantee that the required universals really do exist. I am confident that they do; but my assurance derives from the utility of mathematics in everyday life and in physical science. And this is not as secure, as a priori, as it has been traditional to expect mathematics to be.

Truthmaker is important for the foundations of mathematics, then, because it promises to supply a stock of universals—a subject-matter for mathematics—a priori.

In particular, Truthmaker motivates the key axiom of set theory, the so-called comprehension axiom. Truthmaker requires that when something is true, there must be things whose existence makes it true; and this requirement is neatly met for the statements of set theory. The existence of a set, A say, and one of its members, *a* say, is quite sufficient to make true the statement that:

> *a* is a member of the set A.

If we then interpret every mathematical statement as *classifying* some things, as belonging to some set, then we have furnished all mathematics with truthmakers.

Thus, a hankering after a priori foundations leads to Truthmaker; and Truthmaker supplies one motive for the modern tendency to construe all mathematics in set theory.

There are other motives behind set theory. The recognition of recurrence is, in my opinion, sufficient to support the existence of a wide range of universals, including sets. Yet it would be nice to have a second support from Truthmaker; and if this second support could add a degree of a priori assurance, that would be better yet.

And so I will explore Truthmaker. As will emerge, Truthmaker can be used to generate several sorts of things, each of which has some claim to inherit the title of 'universals', or at least to do the work which universals have traditionally been expected to perform. And each has some claim, thereby, to supply the subject-matter of mathematics.

Correspondence theories of truth breed legions of recalcitrant philosophical problems. For this reason I have sometimes tried to stop believing in the Truthmaker axiom. Yet I have never really succeeded. Without some such axiom, I find I have no adequate anchor to hold me from drifting onto the shoals of some sort of pragmatism or idealism. And that is altogether uncongenial to me; I am a congenital realist about almost everything, as long as it is compatible with some sort of naturalism or physicalism, loosely construed.

But whatever your prejudices about the correspondence theory of truth, it is important to come to terms with Truthmaker if we are to get a rounded picture of traditional theories of universals, and of the interface between mathematics and metaphysics.

In mathematics, we deal with mathematical entities like numbers, which are not easily pinned down in space or time and which, I will argue, are to be conceived as universals, in the sense of recurrences. But there is another focus of interest in mathematics, centring around mathematical *functions*. And functions also hook up with the theory of universals, though in a somewhat different manner. Functions constitute one of the aspects under which *relations* present themselves to us, and under this aspect they link very closely with the Truthmaker axiom.

Consider for instance the function, call it f, which maps any number x onto a number $y = f(x)$ which is the square of x, that is which is equal to the product of x times x:

$$y = f(x) = x^2.$$

This function can be graphed, as in Fig. 42. Every point on the graph has distance x from the y-axis, and distance y from the x-axis. And for every point on the curve, $y = x^2$. This means that the *proportion* between the distance y and the distance x, is the same as the proportion between x and a given distance designated as the *unit*. The curve thus determines all pairs of distances which stand in a particular relation of proportion—and it thereby also determines all pairs of real numbers x and y for which $y = x^2$.

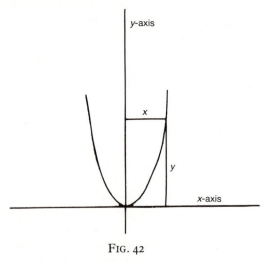

FIG. 42

A graph, or curve, is an object. It is an aggregate (or set) of points, and each of these points determines a pair of distances, or real numbers. So the curve is an object which is very intimately related to the *function* $y = x^2$—and hence to the *relation* between each real number and its square. Modern mathematics has been permeated by set theory; and it is worth remembering that this has its roots in the intimate connections between functions and their graphs. 'Universals' seem to have been supplanted, in modern mathematics, by 'objects'—graphs or sets—which stand in for them. In fact the term *function* is used ambiguously in current mathematics, sometimes for a relationship which holds between numbers, and sometimes for the object—the curve, or set of points, or set of ordered pairs of real numbers—which that relationship determines. But more of this later.

For the moment, the crucial thing to note about functions is the close connection between functions and truths. The function $y = x^2$

will pair a number $x = 2$ say, with another number $y = 4$, just when a certain proposition involving 2 and 4 is true: that $4 = 2 \times 2$. There are many truths involving the same function:

$$4 = 2 \times 2$$
$$16 = 4 \times 4$$
$$25 = 5 \times 5 \ldots \text{etc.}$$

All these truths concern different numbers; but they all concern the same function—the same relationship between numbers.

This connection between functions and truths is quite general. For any function mapping an 'argument' x onto a 'value' y, there will be corresponding truths about how each such y is related to the corresponding x. The function is a single thing, a One, which enters into Many distinct truths. These truths require truthmakers, and their truthmakers 'have something in common'. A function is this 'something in common' among the many truthmakers for many truths. To understand the role of functions in mathematics, we need to understand the Truthmaker axiom. That axiom generates the *existence* of objects, from *truth*. And that is exactly what mathematics does when *functions* are construed as *objects*—whether sets of ordered pairs ('extensions'), or sets of points, or graphs, or whatever.

Let us probe the Truthmaker axiom further. What precisely does it require? It requires that when something is true, there must be something in the world which *makes* it true. But what is it for something to 'make' something true? Consider a potter who makes a pot: Is he or she the truthmaker for the truth that there is a pot? No, not in the relevant sense. A truthmaker should 'make' something true, not in a causal sense, but rather, in what is presumably a logical sense. A truthmaker is that in virtue of which something is true.

And yet we should not rest content with an explanation which turns on the notion of *virtue*! I urge that what the Truthmaker axiom is really saying is this: Whenever something is true, there must be something whose existence entails that it is true. The 'making' in 'making true' is essentially logical entailment.

Logical entailment is deeply mysterious—and this can hardly be stressed too much—but at least it is, to a much greater extent than 'virtue', something ubiquitous and unavoidable. And that is the best sort of mysterious notion in which to couch a foundational axiom like Truthmaker. I am grateful to my colleague John Fox for urging an entailment formulation of a Truthmaker axiom. I was impressed by the way in which, by attributing this as a shared presupposition among the medieval scholastic philosophers, he managed to transform ancient debates which seemed formlessly bewildering into much more sharply focused and productive puzzles.

Entailment may not be all there is to truthmaking. Not every case of entailment will be a case of truthmaking. But, I claim, every case of truthmaking will be a case of entailment. Perhaps we should formulate truthmaker more delicately, as: 'Whenever something is true, there must be something whose existence entails *in an appropriate way* that it is true.' This leaves much to be desired, but the main point is that unless the existence of a thing does entail a truth, *that thing* cannot be an adequate or complete truthmaker for that truth.

This can be illustrated as follows. Suppose there to be something which is proposed as a truthmaker for some truth. And suppose it is admitted that the existence of that thing does not entail the truth in question. This means that it is logically possible for that thing still to exist, even if what is actually true had not been true. In the actual world, *a* exists and A is true, say; but in some other possible world *a* might still exist, even though A is not true. There must surely be some difference between these two possible worlds! They are clearly different in that A is true in one but not in the other. So there must be something in one of these worlds which is lacking in the other, and which accounts for this difference in truth. Such at any rate is the intuition behind Truthmaker. If something is true, then *there must be*, that is to say, there must *exist*, something which makes the actual world different from how it would have been if this had not been true.

Thus phrased, Truthmaker rests heavily on the two notions of *entailment* and *truth*. I will make a few remarks to indicate the roles I see these notions as playing here. First, entailment. I suppose that entailment is to be a relation between propositions (whatever they are). Truthmaker should not be construed as saying that an *object* entails a truth; rather, it requires that the proposition *that that object exists* entails the truth in question.

I will not say much about what sorts of things I take propositions to be. As I see it, that would be peripheral to my current concerns. In fact, 'propositions' may be appearing here as no more than a convenient manner of speech, rather than as genuine protagonists in the drama. We can restate Truthmaker so that 'propositions' fade into the wings. What Truthmaker says is: 'For each truth A there must be something *a* such that, *necessarily, if a exists then A is true*'.

This formulation still features the attribution of *truth* to something. What sort of entity is this thing, A, to which we attribute the property of truth? What sort of thing is a *truth-bearer*? And what sort of property is this thing, truth, which is borne by truth-bearers?

I will side-step these problems as best I can. The force behind Truthmaker lies deeper than worries about the nature of truth and of truth-bearers. The term 'truth' makes its appearance here largely to facilitate generality of exposition. If we focus on just one particular truth, then the guts of Truthmaker can be stated without even using the term 'truth', or any equivalent. Consider for instance the truth that the Parthenon is on the Acropolis. Truthmaker requires that there must be some things such that, *necessarily, if these things exist then the Parthenon is on the Acropolis*. Thus stated, we have made no explicit mention of either propositions or truth. (Leave the analysis of the residue—'necessarily, if . . . then . . .'—for another occasion.)

I introduce Truthmaker as a way of drawing out one of the major traditional sources of theories of universals, a traditional source which is generally stated in semantic terms, in terms involving notions like 'meaning', 'reference', and 'truth'. Universals have been expected to provide a solution to the problem of 'common names'—or better, a solution to the 'problem of predication'. Thus conceived, universals are supposed to be the sorts of things in the world which correspond to predicates. And, it is argued, a predicate cannot just refer to another object of the same sort that the subject-term refers to: otherwise a sentence would be merely a list of names. But a sentence is not just a list of names; a sentence is true or false. Hence what corresponds to a predicate must be something which plays a distinctive role in generating or constituting a truth.

This problem of predication is a mushy one. But I am trying to direct Truthmaker in such a way as to side-step, as far as possible, semantic issues like the problem of predication. The guts of Truthmaker lie in metaphysics rather than in language. They lie in the space between *objects* and *facts*. There would still be a question about what the world is like, and what there must *be* in order for it to be like that, even if there were no language or mind in which to formulate this question or answer it.

19   Truth and Essence

THERE are some truths for which the Truthmaker axiom is not very difficult to satisfy—some truths which it is not very hard to supply with truthmakers.

A truthmaker is simply an object whose existence entails a truth. So consider for instance the truth *that Hypatia*, a camel I met in Warrandyte, *exists*. It is not hard to find a truthmaker for this truth. The existence of Hypatia trivially entails this truth. And so Hypatia serves as an adequate truthmaker for the truth that Hypatia exists.

Unless your natural, essentialist urges have been thoroughly repressed, you will be inclined to agree that there are many other truths which can also be supplied with a straightforward, if somewhat trivial, truthmaker. Some people would leap immediately to a theory which says that what makes something true is a special sort of entity called a fact, or situation, or state of affairs. I will look at theories of that sort all in good time. But for the moment I want to point out that, in the case of some truths, there is no need to posit anything like a 'fact' if all we are aiming to do is to satisfy Truthmaker. Consider for instance the truth *that Hypatia is a camel*. I assume that the Hypatia I met was indeed a camel. And I also assume that there could not have been anything which was not a camel, and yet which was nevertheless Hypatia. And so, in every possible world in which Hypatia exists at all, it is true that Hypatia is a camel. It follows that Hypatia is such that, necessarily, *if she exists then it is true that Hypatia is a camel*. So Hypatia is an adequate truthmaker for the truth that Hypatia is a camel.

We can generalise this to all so-called essential predications. An individual will always be an adequate truthmaker for any truth which involves only the predication of things which are part of the *essence* of that individual.

A property forms part of the essence of an individual when loss of that property would transform the individual into another, numerically distinct individual. In other words, something forms part of the essence of an individual when it is something the individual could not have lacked. Then the existence of the individual will logically entail that the individual has all the things that are essential to it. And so the existence of the individual will logically entail all essential truths about it. Any individual is thus always an adequate truthmaker for all truths about its essence.

Other truths attribute qualities which an object may have at some times and not at others, qualities which are not part of the object's essence. In such a case, it is true that the object has the quality, but the object could have existed even if it had not had the quality. Hence the *existence* of that object does not entail the *truth* that it has that quality. The object does not, by itself, serve as an adequate truthmaker. The truthmaker axiom urges us to admit the existence of something else—a quality—which exists, in addition to the object which has it.

Pure mathematics and applied mathematics differ crucially in the nature of the truths with which they deal. In pure mathematics, the truths are generally essential ones. For instance when we say '17 is a prime number', the quality we ascribe to 17 is part of its essence: the number 17 could not have lacked this property without ceasing to be the number that it is. So Truthmaker puts no pressure on us, in this case, to admit the existence of anything over and above the object. There is no pressure on us to admit the existence of the quality of primeness in addition to the number 17.

It is worth noting here a relationship between Truthmaker and set theory. In the early days of set theory, it was tempting to advance as self-evident what is known as an unrestricted comprehension axiom. In effect, this axiom claims that whenever something is *true* of an object, there will *exist* something else, in addition to the object, namely there will exist the set of all the things of which this is true. Note that this is in an important respect a stronger claim than Truthmaker. It requires that, even when what is true of an object is part of its essence, we can still infer the existence of something (a set) over and above the object itself. The Truthmaker axiom has the same importance for mathematics as the comprehension axiom: it promises to generate, a priori, all the objects we need to furnish the subject matter for mathematics. But Truthmaker is more modest: the comprehension axiom generates objects from both essential and accidental truths, whereas Truthmaker generates them only from accidental truths.

Given that pure mathematics concerns only essential truths, this means that Truthmaker does not generate mathematical objects from pure mathematics alone.

In applied mathematics, in contrast, Truthmaker does press us into admitting the existence of mathematical properties in addition to the objects which display them. But more of this later. Truthmaker presents us with a few problem we need to deal with even before we turn from essential truths to the even more problematic class of accidental truths.

Consider now another example. Let A be the truth that *there are camels*. Once again, we need look no further than Hypatia in search of a truthmaker, the existence of Hypatia entails the truth of A—the existence of Hypatia is a sufficient condition for the truth of A. So Hypatia is *a* truthmaker for A. But notice that the existence of Hypatia is not a necessary condition for the truth of A. Hypatia is one truthmaker, but there are others, and there could have been others again.

It is worth keeping this in mind when thinking about Truthmaker. The Truthmaker axiom should not be construed as requiring a unique truthmaker for each truth. So it might be wise to rephrase it slightly, thus: Whenever something is true, there must be some thing *or things* whose existence entails that truth.

There is in fact a second reason why it is wise to allow for a plurality of truthmakers. There are cases where the existence of several things, together, entails a given truth, whereas the existence of just some of them would not. Let B be the truth that *there are at least two camels*. The existence of *both* Hypatia *and* Theodora entails the truth; but the existence of Hypatia does not, and nor does the existence of Theodora.

You might argue that it is really the existence of some (single) thing, called *the pair* of camels, Hypatia and Theodora, which entails the truth of B. Yet it is not necessary, in the present context, to summon up the existence of any such thing as a 'pair' of camels, in addition to the two camels themselves. We can satisfy the fundamental urges underlying Truthmaker simply by making the slightly weaker claim that the existence of Hypatia *and* Theodora entails the truth of B. So Hypatia and Theodora, as a plurality, are truthmakers for B.

The considerations raised so far prompt us to revise Truthmaker in only a relatively minor respect, to allow for non-unique and plural truthmakers. Yet there are other truths which force a deeper revision.

Consider again the truth that there are at least two camels. Now extend this numerical claim to embrace more and more camels: 'There are at least a thousand camels', 'There are at least a hundred thousand camels', . . . and so on. I do not know how long you can continue in this manner before truths give way to falsehoods. Suppose there are exactly N camels altogether. Then consider the truth:

(N): There are at least N camels.

The existence of all the camels there are will entail this truth. So *camels* constitute adequate truthmakers for (N).

But now compare (N) with the following truth:

(N−): There are fewer than (N + 1) camels.

This is a truth, so it requires a truthmaker, or truthmakers. The Truthmaker axiom requires us to say that there is some thing or things whose existence entails that there are no more than N camels. Yet what sort of thing or things could possibly be such that their existence entails that there are no more camels?

Some may be tempted to draw upon the notion of facts here, and say that it is the existence of the fact that there are no more camels, which entails (N−). But I set that aside for the time being.

In a specific sort of theology, God might serve as a truthmaker for (N−). A Leibniz might argue, for instance, that necessarily God creates the best of all possible worlds, and that a world with (N + 1) camels would be less perfect than one with only N camels, and that hence, necessarily, if God exists then there are fewer than N + 1 camels. Yet surely Truthmaker had better not rest on so idiosyncratic a theology.

The truth (N−), we may note, involves negation. And negative truths were, notoriously, trouble-makers which plagued the development of Russell's philosophy of logical atomism: see for instance Pears (1972).

In the face of this problem we might choose to revise Truthmaker somehow, rather than choosing to introduce entities of new sorts, especially tailored to satisfy the unrevised, naïve Truthmaker. And indeed, that is what I propose that we do.

One sort of revision worth trying would be one which places restrictions on the *scope* of Truthmaker. We might divide truths into two sorts: say *atomic* truths and *molecular* truths. And we might then revise Truthmaker so that it claims only that *for any atomic truth* there must be some thing or things whose existence entails that it is true. We might then go on to tell a subsidiary story about how a molecular truth derives its truth indirectly from the atomic truths. The sort of theory we might arrive at, by revising Truthmaker along these lines, would be something like Tarski's celebrated theory of truth—see for instance Tarski (1956).

I propose, however, to cut across the problems besetting such a project by weakening the Truthmaker axiom in a somewhat different manner. I propose to weaken Truthmaker by drawing upon the currently very productive notion of *supervenience*.

One sort of thing is said to be supervenient on another when *you could not have any difference in things of the first sort unless there were some difference in things of the second sort.*

For instance a painting may be described as gloomy, or violent, or tranquil, and so forth. The gloominess of a painting will, plausibly, be supervenient on physical facts about the colour and spatial distribution of bits of paint—and perhaps on their relationships to human agents. You could not have two paintings, one say violent and the other tranquil, without some difference in the colour and distribution of the bits of paint on those two paintings.

A topic of current debate concerns the question of whether facts about the mind, about thoughts and feelings, are supervenient on physical facts about the body. Could you have two people who were physically indistinguishable, and yet who experienced different feelings and had different thoughts? If not, then the mind is supervenient on the body.

To these applications of the notion of supervenience, I wish to add another. The essence of Truthmaker, I urge, is the idea that truth is supervenient on being: that you could not have any difference in what things are true unless there were some difference in what things exist.

Consider again the truth $(N-)$, that there are fewer than $(N + 1)$ camels. Compare the actual world, in which this is true, with some other world, in which it is false:

Actual World	*Other World*
$c_1, c_2 \ldots, c_N$	$d_1, d_2, \ldots, d_N, d_{(N + 1)}$

These are things in the actual world which make it true that there are at least N camels; but there is, I submit, nothing in the actual world whose existence entails that there are no more camels. In the other world, in contrast, there *are* things whose existence entails that (N) is *false*. The camels $d_1, \ldots, d_{(N + 1)}$ are *falsemakers* for $(N-)$. So they are truthmakers for the negation of $(N-)$. In order to change $(N-)$ from a truth into a falsehood, it is necessary to alter the inventory of things in the world. We must at least add an extra thing, to yield a truthmaker for the negation of $(N-)$, before we can convert $(N-)$ from a truth into a falsehood.

Any attempt to weaken Truthmaker, without totally evacuating it of content, will have to preserve, as a central core, the idea that truth is supervenient on being. So I offer the following, supervenience formulation:

> *Truthmaker*
> If something is true, then it would not be possible for it to be false unless either certain things were to exist which don't, or else certain things had not existed which do.

This principle is not hard to satisfy when applied to truths involving essential predications. However, even when weakened to a supervenience thesis, Truthmaker is not so easy to satisfy when applied to accidental predications.

Consider for instance the truth that Hypatia is thirsty. The existence of Hypatia is not sufficient to entail that Hypatia is thirsty. So Truthmaker requires that *either* there is some thing or things in addition to Hypatia such that, if they had not existed then Hypatia would not have been thirsty; *or else*, if there had been certain other things which do not actually exist, then Hypatia would not have been thirsty.

What could such a thing or things be? For Hypatia to be thirsty, we might suggest, there must not only be Hypatia, there must also be such a thing as *thirst*. And thirst is a universal. The craving to satisfy Truthmaker thus urges us towards a recognition of the existence of universals. Universals are the sorts of things whose existence is required to plug the gap between individual things and accidental truths about those things.

Tradition has required universals to be the sorts of things which enable us to satisfy Truthmaker. I will argue, however, that if universals are fashioned in such a manner as to genuinely satisfy Truthmaker, then there are certain other things which they simply cannot do as well. In particular, they cannot then be the sorts of things which underlie Recurrence—the sorts of things which may be aptly conceived as a One over Many.

To demonstrate this, I propose to set out an inconsistent tetrad: four conditions which cannot all be satisfied together. Universals have been expected to satisfy all four. So the traditional conception of a universal has constituted a logically inconsistent package deal. In order to reconstruct a consistent package, at least one of the four conditions must be abandoned. The various traditional theories of universals can be seen as arising from different choices about which of the four conditions to abandon. We can in fact construct a taxonomy of theories of universals by asking of each such theory precisely which of the four conditions it abandons.

I will call this inconsistent tetrad the Fox paradox, since there is no aspect of it which I am confident was not at least partly borrowed from John Fox, except for my having chosen to present it by speaking (explicitly) of possible worlds, and my having chosen to carve it up into an inconsistent tetrad.

20   The Fox paradox

SOME aggregates of pebbles may have the property of 'being arranged as a square grid'. One of these aggregates might be called a. The existence of a is not sufficient by itself for the truth that a is arranged as a square grid. Hence Truthmaker requires that something else must be present, in addition to the aggregate a of pebbles, in order for that truth to hold of it. Wrapped up within this 'something else', we will find the subject-matter of mathematics. The 'something else' which makes a a square grid may be shared by another, numerically distant batch of pebbles, b say. So this 'something else' is a universal. And it inextricably involves numbers: the number of rows in a or b must be the same as the number of columns. Numbers are universals, and are constituents within complex universals such as that of 'being arranged as a square grid'.

In exploring the nature of numbers, I will probe the status of universals; and, in so doing, I will shift to a more mnemonic illustration. Let a now be taken to be an Arctic fox, Albina, and let the property in question be that of whiteness. (It is quite likely that a fox is really just an aggregate of things which are more complex than mere pebbles, and that whiteness is really just a pattern which is instantiated by that aggregate, and which is more subtle and elaborate than the mere property of being arranged as a square grid. Whiteness is less patently mathematical than squareness, but it is more vivid and it adequately illustrates all the problems I wish to discuss here.)

Thus, suppose there is an Arctic fox called Albina, or a for short; and let A be the truth, that Albina has whiteness. This is an accidental predication. Albina must exist for A to be true, but the existence of Albina is not, by itself, sufficient to entail that it is true.

Truthmaker requires that there could not be a difference in what is true unless there were a difference in what exists. This implies that at least one of the following two options obtains. The first option is this: there is some thing or things such that, if A were false, then some of those things would not exist. The second option is this: if A were false, then something would have to exist which does not actually exist.

I assume A to be a truth for which only the first option applies. In fact, what I assume is that there are truths for which the first option applies. For the purposes of illustration, suppose A to be such a truth.

I assume, then, that if A had been false, then some actually existing thing or things would not have existed. This means that the truth of A rests on the existence of some thing or things *whose joint existence entails A*. Albina is one of these things, but her existence alone does not entail A. So there must be some other thing or things—call them α—whose existence together with Albina entails A. Remember that α may be several things, perhaps even an infinite plurality, or it may be just a single thing.

Suppose in addition that there is some other truth, B say, which is of the same sort as A. Let it be an accidental predication of whiteness to another individual, say a polar bear, Bianca, or b for short. Then there will have to be some thing or things, β, whose existence together with b entails the truth B, that Bianca has whiteness.

I assume, further, that A and B are logically independent, so that A could be true even if B were false.

Now consider two possible situations, in one of which both A and B are true, and in the other of which A is true but B is not. Both worlds will need truthmakers for A; but we will not assume yet that the truthmakers for A need to be the same in the two different situations. It could be that what makes A true in the one situation is different from what makes it true in the other situation. So let us *call* the truthmakers for A, in the other possible situation, c and γ, without begging the question either way as to whether a = c, or α = γ.

The case is slightly different for truth B. It is true in one situation, but not in the other. In one situation, therefore, there will need to be truthmakers for B; call them b and β. But in the other situation these two cannot both exist. Since they together constitute truthmakers for B, if they both existed then this would entail that B was true. So at least one must fail to exist. But the other could still exist; so in case we need to consider the case where one of them does still exist, let us introduce the name d as a dummy for whatever we might need to refer to in a situation where A is true but B is false. If this situation were one which contained nothing but the truthmakers for A, then we would have to take d to refer to one of those truthmakers for A. The main thing to remember is that I am trying to beg as few questions as possible.

We can then set out the two possible situations as in Fig. 43. On the left we have a description of what is in fact the case. On the right we have a description of how things could have been but aren't. The schematic letters are to be taken as non-committally as possible; thus

Actual World   Other World

```
┌─────────────────────────────┐      ┌─────────────────────────────┐
│  A is true;                 │      │  A is true;                 │
│  a exists;                  │      │  c exists;                  │
│  α exists or exist.         │      │  γ exists or exist.         │
│                             │      │                             │
│  B is true;                 │      │  B is false;                │
│  b exists;                  │      │  d exists.                  │
│  β exists or exist.         │      │                             │
└─────────────────────────────┘      └─────────────────────────────┘
```

FIG. 43

for instance the use of distinct letters a and c, b and d, should not be taken to prejudge the question whether or not a = c or b = d, or even whether c = d. I do assume though, that a ≠ b.

So far, the descriptions of the Actual World and Other World embody only a few relatively innocent assumptions, in addition to Truthmaker. The description given of the two worlds presupposes that A and B are logically independent accidental predications. It is also supposed that in the actual world, a and α serve as truthmakers for A, and b and β serve as truthmakers for B. And if A were still true though B were false, then there would still need to be truthmakers for A, though not for B.

To make explicit the way Truthmaker applies to the case of Albina and Bianca, I will lay out the following principle of:

Sufficiency
The existence of a and α entails that A;
the existence of b and β entails that B;
the existence of c and γ entails that A.

To this principle of Sufficiency, I will add principles which flow from the idea that A and B are accidental predications. The accidentality of these truths would seem to imply that the very same individual b could still have existed even if B were false, so that b = d. That is it would seem that Bianca could still have existed even if she had not had whiteness. Similarly, Albina could still have existed even if Bianca had not had whiteness, so that a = c. Hence we can assert the following principle of:

Accidents
a = c
b = d.

The next principle I will add is also based on the assumption that A and B are logically independent. The truth of A need not be affected by the truth or falsity of B; and furthermore *that in virtue of which* A is true need not be affected by the truth or falsity of B. This yields the principle of:

Robustness

$\alpha = \gamma$.

The last member of my inconsistent tetrad is the one which links Truthmakers with Recurrences:

One Over Many

$\alpha = \beta$.

These four principles lead to a logical contradiction, as follows:

(i) By Accidents, b = d; and so we can infer that b exists in the Other World.

(ii) By One Over Many together with Robustness, we get $\beta = \alpha = \gamma$; so we can infer that β exists in the Other World.

(iii) So both b and β exist in the Other World. By Sufficiency, the existence of b and β entails that B is true in the Other World.

(iv) Yet B is false in the Other World, by hypothesis. Hence we have derived a contradiction: B is both true and false in the Other World. So something has got to give.

This paradox is a little less crisp than I would like. There are quite a few threads which need to be pulled together to get a contradiction; so there are many ways we could try to block the paradox. The four principles I have selected and labelled are not quite the only assumptions used in setting the paradox. Nevertheless, they are the key elements used in deriving a contradiction. Given any theory of universals you may set before me, I want to know *which* of these four principles that theory denies. I doubt very much whether a satisfactory, consistent theory could be put together without denying at least one of the four.

21   Counterparts and Accidents

IN the Fox paradox, the two key principles are Sufficiency and One Over Many. The first of these ensures that universals play a distinctive sort of role as *truthmakers*; the other links universals with *recurrences*. Both of these are essential to the traditional conception of universals. So it is worth exploring the possibility of finding a consistent theory which satisfies both Sufficiency and One Over Many.

If we preserve both Sufficiency and One Over Many, then we must abandon one of the other two members of the inconsistent Fox tetrad: we must abandon either Accidents or Robustness. Let us look first at Accidents.

Can we block the Fox contradiction by abandoning Accidents: by denying that a = c and b = d? That is to say, could we block the contradiction by saying that if Bianca had not had whiteness, then Bianca and Albina would not have existed?

A theory of this character was held by Leibniz, for instance in the following passage from his *Discourse on Metaphysics* (see Lucas and Grint, 1953):

But . . . whence comes it that this man will assuredly commit this sin? The reply is easy, it is that otherwise it would not be this man.

As the saying goes: 'A different act—a different Adam!'; no one could have done any differently from what they did without being a different person. And recently, D. K. Lewis (1968, 1986) has defended a similar theory.

On a theory of this kind, d cannot be literally identical with *b*, since there is something which is true of b but not of d—B is true of b but not of d. That is, d cannot be Bianca, since Bianca has whiteness and d does not.

The relationship between b and d, between Bianca (our Bianca, the actual Bianca) and d, must then be something other than strict identity. Lewis's apt phrase is: d is the *counterpart* of b. This means that d is importantly (sufficiently) *similar* to b—and that nothing else in the Other World is more similar to b than d is. Because d, in the Other World, is rather like the actual Bianca, and because nothing else in the Other World pre-empts d's claim to 'stand in for' the actual Bianca, we may well be tempted to apply the same name, 'Bianca', to both b and d. But we should remember that, strictly speaking, there are two distinct individuals involved, the actual Bianca, b, and the Other-Worldly Bianca, d; and b ≠ d.

When we say something could have been true of Bianca—for instance that Bianca could have had some colour other than white—it is tempting to interpret this as meaning that in some possible world *Bianca* exists without having whiteness. On a counterpart theory, however, what is really the case is that the actual Bianca has a *counterpart* which has a colour other than white. We can say an individual 'could have had different properties', just when the individual's *counterparts* do have different properties. The individual is not, however, literally, numerically identical with any other-worldly individual which has different properties in some other possible world.

Let us explore the consequences which a counterpart theory would have for the Fox paradox. The first thing to notice is, of course, that a counterpart theory denies Accidents. The principle of Accidents was used as one of the essential steps in deriving the Fox contradiction. Hence it would seem that a counterpart theory blocks the contradiction just by denying Accidents. There then seems to be no need to deny Sufficiency or One Over Many as well. And thus, it might seem, a counterpart theory can support a full-blooded theory of universals. Yet let us probe a little deeper.

It is, indeed, easy for a counterpart theory to satisfy Sufficiency as formulated so far. In fact, it is all too easy. That is to say, it is all too easy to find a thing or things whose existence entails that A and B are true. If A or B had not been true, then a or b could not have existed—that is what a counterpart theory says. And so the existence of a or b logically entails that A and B are true. Hence Albina, by herself, is an adequate truthmaker for the truth that Albina has whiteness. Similarly, Bianca is an adequate truthmaker for the truth that Bianca has whiteness. There is no need to supplement Albina and Bianca by introducing any further thing or things α and β. So we may simply set $\alpha = a$ and $\beta = b$. And then this conflicts with One Over Many, which requires, we may remember, that $\alpha = \beta$.

To preserve One Over Many, we must thus set $\alpha \neq a$ and $\beta \neq b$; but then α (= β) is completely idle as far as truthmaking for A or B are concerned.

Counterpart theory *seems* to solve the problem of accidental predications; and the way it seems to do so is by the drastic measure of denying that there are any! *Every* property of Albina is an essential property, in the sense that Albina herself could not have existed without any one of her actual properties. Once all predications have been reduced to essential predications, we will find it easy, all too easy, to satisfy Truthmaker.

However, if we pursue counterpart theory a little further, some oddities begin to emerge. Notice that if Bianca had not had whiteness, then on a counterpart theory, not only would Bianca herself not have existed, but Albina too would not have existed. There would be various things which would be true of the Other Worldly Albina, c, which are not true of the actual Albina, a. So not only does the existence of the actual Bianca, b, entail the truth of B, but in addition the existence of the actual Albina, a, entails the truth of B. That is to say, the existence of Albina entails that Bianca has whiteness!

The trouble with using counterpart theory to solve the Fox paradox, is that if deployed in a way which blocks the contradiction, then it plays havoc with the principle of Sufficiency. It evacuates Sufficiency of all the content it was intended to have. On a counterpart theory, the objects a and b exist in the Actual World *and no other*, they are 'world-bound'. Consequently, the only possible world where a and b exist will be the Actual World, a world in which A is true and B is true, and all sorts of other things are true as well. And so the existence of a or b, or anything else in the Actual World, will entail the truth of A or B, or anything else that is true in the Actual World.

Counterpart theory, taken flatfootedly, solves the Fox paradox by denying that there are any accidental predications—under one interpretation of 'accidental predications'. Yet when applied in this way, it avoids the contradiction only by trivializing Sufficiency, and making One Over Many completely idle. By itself it does not generate a decent theory of *universals*.

I wish to stress, however, that this is no deficiency in counterpart theory itself, properly understood. It remains an open question whether a counterpart theory could be supplemented in ways which would yield an adequate theory of universals.

To begin with, consider again the notion of accidental predications. It is tempting to describe counterpart theory by saying that it construes all properties as 'essential', and none as 'accidental'—on the grounds that no individual could have existed with different properties. But a more charitable choice of terminology is also possible. We can call a property of an individual 'accidental' when the individual has some *counterparts* who lack the property.

In general, when interpreting counterpart theory, one must keep in mind the fact that whenever we are inclined to talk of identity across possible worlds—whenever we are inclined to talk of what some individual *would* have been like in other circumstances—the counterpart theorist is going to speak not of a single individual or of identity across worlds, but rather, of the *counterpart relation* holding among a plurality of individuals.

This must be applied across the board. And, in particular, it must be applied to the interpretation of Truthmaker. A counterpart theorist must not interpret Truthmaker as requiring only that truth is supervenient on what individuals, strictly construed, *exist*. That makes it too trivial. Rather, a counterpart theorist's Truthmaker should read rather more like this:

Counterpart Truthmaker
If something is true, then it would not be possible for it to be false unless either certain things were to exist which have no actual counterparts, or else certain actual things were to have no existing counterparts.

Continuing in the same vein, we should recast Sufficiency as requiring:

Counterpart Sufficiency
The existence of counterparts of a and α entails the truth of A; the existence of counterparts of b and β entails the truth of B; the existence of counterparts of c and γ entails the truth of A.

If we now go on to replace Accidents and Robustness by the claims that c is the counterpart of a, that d is the counterpart of b, and that γ is the counterpart of α, then the Fox contradiction will simply re-emerge.

We do not need to decide here whether to accept a counterpart theory. The solution to the Fox paradox will be orthogonal to counterpart theory. If we can find a solution which works outside a counterpart theory, we may then, if we wish, simply map that solution into the counterpart framework.

22 Property-instances

THE views I am going to explore next emerge from the attempt to preserve Sufficiency, and hence Truthmaker. We cannot hold all four of the key propositions in the Fox paradox. If we are to preserve Sufficiency, we must thus deny at least one of the others. Denying Accidents only postpones the paradox, and does not solve it. that leaves us to consider the denial of Robustness or of One Over Many. I will take One Over Many first; the denial of Robustness will emerge as just a variant on theories which deny One Over Many.

Suppose we deny One Over Many, we deny that $\alpha = \beta$. What makes it true that Albina has whiteness? The suggested answer will be: it is the existence of Albina together with the existence of Albina's whiteness. The truth, A, that Albina has whiteness, is thus made true by the existence of the two joint truthmakers, a (Albina), and α (Albina's whiteness). Similarly, what makes B true is the exisence of Bianca, b, and Bianca's whiteness, β. But Albina's whiteness is not numerically identical with Bianca's whiteness: $\alpha \neq \beta$. Albina's whiteness may be very similar to Bianca's, and so we may be tempted to say that they have 'the same' colour. But this should only mean that we assign the same exact shade to those two whitenesses. However similar they are, however exactly they match, they are two numerically distinct entities.

Albina's whiteness is where Albina is; Bianca's whiteness is where Bianca is. This by itself, I protest, does not prove that there are two numerically distinct whitenesses in the two different places. One might well wish to say that one and the same property exists in two distinct locations. But what is being suggested here is the possibility that the whitenesses of Albina and Bianca may indeed be just as numerically distinct as Albina and Bianca themselves. This proposal not only has the tempting feature of reinforcing our deep-seated prejudices about locality—our prejudice against allowing anything to be in two places at once—but also this proposal promises to block the Fox contradiction without conflicting with Truthmaker.

The way Sufficiency is satisfied by a property-instance theory is, in fact, by reconstruing what was supposed to be an accidental predication in such a way as to transform it into an essential one. And essentialist predications are readily supplied with truthmakers, as we saw earlier in the case of truths like 'Hypatia is a camel.'

The way an apparently accidental predication is reduced to an essential one, is as follows. We begin with predication like 'Albina has whiteness.' We then suppose there to be such a thing as Albina's whiteness. The existence of this thing (together with Albina) *entails* that Albina has whiteness. But this will only hold provided it is *essential* to Albina's whiteness *that it is had by Albina*. Albina's whiteness cannot exist without Albina; and Bianca could not have Albina's whiteness, nor Albina Bianca's. Otherwise Sufficiency would fail. Hence the apparently accidental predication on Albina,

'Albina has whiteness'

is in fact equivalent to an essential predication on Albina's whiteness:

'Albina's whiteness is had by Albina.'

And this is made true merely by the existence of Albina's whiteness.

Thus, the existence of Albina's whiteness entails the existence of Albina. We can re-express this by saying Albina's whiteness could not exist without Albina. And this echoes one recurrent theme in traditional theories of universals—that properties, unlike individuals, have only a *dependent existence*.

On this theory, we can preserve not only Sufficiency and Accidents, but also Robustness. If Bianca had not had whiteness, then although β (Bianca's whiteness) would not have existed, this is no reason for saying that α (Albina's whiteness) would not have existed. So we are free to say that $\alpha = \gamma$. That is to say, we are free to say that A could have had exactly the same truthmakers even if B had been false. And this is a very desirable thing to be able to say. It echoes the intuition that since A and B are logically independent truths, one could have been false without affecting what makes the other one true.

The theory of property-instances is neat; it preserves Sufficiency, Accidents, and Robustness. The cost is only the loss of One Over Many. And yet this cost is high enough, I think. It is dubious whether truthmakers which fail to satisfy One Over Many could appropriately be called *universals*.

Yet consider the following variant on the property-instances theory a variant which I call the Taylor twist, since it was brought to my attention by Barry Taylor of Melbourne University. The Taylor twist gives us a way of reconstructing a property-instance theory so that it does satisfy One Over Many, after all.

Suppose there are indeed two distinct truthmakers, α and β, for truths A and B. Then form the *aggregate* of α and β; call this the *sum* of α and β, $(\alpha + \beta)$. This is to be an entity which has α and β as *parts*.

Now consider using this aggregate, $(\alpha + \beta)$, to meet the needs of a theory of universals. Let us see what happens to the Fox paradox if we replace both α and β by the aggregate, $(\alpha + \beta)$. Notice, first, that One Over Many, $\alpha = \beta$, is clearly satisfied, because α and β have both been replaced by the same entity, $(\alpha + \beta)$.

We have thus taken a theory which satisfies Sufficiency, Accidents, and Robustness, and we have now transformed it in such a way as to satisfy One Over Many. But we know in advance that, by making the theory satisfy One Over Many, we will have to also make some compensatory adjustment which subverts at least one of the other three principles. Otherwise the transformed theory will be inconsistent. So which of the other three principles has been subverted by the Taylor twist? It is hoped, not Accidents, since the denial of Accidents will not support a decent theory of universals. Hence the Taylor twist must have undermined either Sufficiency or Robustness.

In choosing whether to reject Sufficiency or Robustness, we will need to choose between two distinct attitudes one may take towards aggregates. Suppose we take an aggregate $(\alpha + \beta)$ to be an entity of such a sort that this same entity *could not have existed if either α or β had not existed*. That is suppose that the whole could not have existed without all its parts. (Within a counterpart theory, this amounts to the claim that any counterpart of a whole must have, as parts, counterparts of all its parts.)

On this construal, the Taylor twist yields a theory which satisfies Sufficiency, but not Robustness.

It satisfies Sufficiency, since the existence of $(\alpha + \beta)$ serves as an adequate truthmaker for both A and B. The existence of $(\alpha + \beta)$ is being supposed to entail the existence of α, and hence the truth of A, and also to entail the existence of β, and hence the truth of B.

But the new theory no longer satisfies Robustness. In order to meet Sufficiency, we have had to say that $(\alpha + \beta)$ could not have existed if β had not existed. But since B is false in the Other World, we must say β does not exist in the Other World. So the truthmaker for A in the Other World, γ, cannot be identical with $(\alpha + \beta)$:

$$\gamma \neq (\alpha + \beta).$$

And yet $(\alpha + \beta)$ is supposed to be the truthmaker for A in the Actual

World: the Taylor twist replaces α by $(\alpha + \beta)$ throughout. So under the Taylor twist, Robustness would become the assertion that $(\alpha + \beta) = \gamma$. And this contradicts the result, $\gamma \neq (\alpha + \beta)$, which we have just derived from the attempt to ensure that aggregates of property-instances do meet the principle of Sufficiency.

Thus, a theory using aggregates of property-instances can satisfy both Sufficiency and One Over Many, but only by abandoning Robustness.

Alternatively, we could preserve both One Over Many and Robustness, but only by abandoning Sufficiency. This option rests on a somewhat different conception of aggregates. Intuitively, it is very natural to think that something which is (plausibly) an aggregate could survive the loss of some of its parts. A heap of beans would not necessarily become a different heap just by the removal of one bean, would it? So similarly we may find it natural to say that the same aggregate of property-instances could still exist, even if some of the property-instances it contains had been absent. There is an aggregate of property-instances in the Actual World, and, *in* the Actual World this aggregate contains both α and β as parts. In the Other World, this same aggregate still exists, yet now it contains α as a part, but it no longer contains β. We may then construe both α and β as referring to this same aggregate; so Robustness is satisfied, $\alpha = \gamma$. And so is One Over Many, $\alpha = \beta$, since both β and α refer to this same aggregate.

It follows that, thus construed, the Taylor twist will flout Sufficiency. The aggregate in question exists in the Actual World, but *its* existence does *not* entail the truth of B. This follows immediately from the fact that this aggregate does exist in the Other World, and yet B is false in that Other World.

Let us sum up the situation so far. A property-instance theory begins by introducing property-instances, and construing them in such a way as to meet the principle of Sufficiency. These are the basic truthmakers for accidental predications. But since they fail One Over Many, they cannot really be called universals. The theory does, however, have the resources for constructing entities—aggregates of property-instances—which do satisfy One Over Many. There are two ways of doing this: one way generates things which fail Sufficiency; the other way generates things which fail Robustness.

And yet neither of these sorts of aggregates really qualifies as a *universal*. A universal, as a *recurrence*, is the sort of thing which can be 'wholly present' in several places at once, that is it can be present in different places without having distinct parts each of which is present in just one of those places and not the other. And this is precisely what aggregates of property-instances are not.

An aggregate's failure to be 'wholly present' in different locations is reflected in the fact that such aggregates *must* violate either Sufficiency or Robustness.

If an aggregate violates Robustness, that entails that this alleged 'one over many' could not have existed if Bianca had not had whiteness. This surely means it is *not* that in virtue of which Albina has whiteness. It is neither an appropriate truthmaker nor a genuine recurrence.

Conversely, if an aggregate is one of the sort which violates Sufficiency, then it is the sort of thing which could still have existed even if Bianca had not had whiteness. So it is surely *not* that in virtue of which Bianca has whiteness. It is neither an appropriate truthmaker nor a genuine recurrence.

I conclude that a property-instance theory can block the Fox contradiction, but not in a way which generates a viable theory of *universals*. Defenders of a property-instance theory might well argue that the *illusion* of recurrence, of One Over Many, is generated by the tendency to think of a whole class of distinct, but qualitatively matching property-instances, *as if* it were a single thing present in each instance. But properly understood, on a property-instance theory there are no genuine universals.

Property-instance theories, then, do rather well at satisfying Truthmaker. And they can even take some steps towards explaining away the appearance of Recurrence. If the *only* motive for positing universals were the desire to satisfy Truthmaker, and to solve the problem of predication, then perhaps it would be rational to opt for a property-instances theory.

Yet the moral I wish to draw is less partisan. It is only that universals should not be expected to play any distinctive role in truthmaking.

The Fox paradox shows us that genuine universals which satisfy One Over Many cannot be truthmakers in the sort of way which meets the principle of Sufficiency. Yet this by no means shows us that there are no universals. At most, it undermines one, semantic, motive some people have had for believing in universals. But there is another powerful motive for at least exploring the possibility of a theory of universals, namely the recognition that the opposing view rests on nothing but unargued prejudices about *locality*. By freeing ourselves from those prejudices, one of the benefits we may reap, in particular, is a viable realist philosophy of mathematics.

The moral of the Fox paradox is worth keeping in mind when thinking about the philosophy of mathematics. The moral of the Fox paradox is that *universals* must not be expected to play any distinctive role in truthmaking. And yet current mathematics has been grounded in set theory; and set theory generates mathematical entities out of something very close to the presumption that every truth requires a truthmaker. *Functions*, too, are generated in mathematics from something very close to that same presumption. And yet truthmakers are not the best source from which to draw the subject-matter of mathematics. The sorts of entities which emerge from Truthmaker—that is from logic and semantics—are not universals. And the ways in which they differ from universals make them ill-suited to serve as the subject-matter for mathematics.

23   Robinson's Merger

WHEN in the right mood, it can seem simply obvious that one can see the same, numerically identical, patterns, properties, and so forth, on different occasions, and at widely scattered locations. But even if it is not obvious, the contrary view, which enforces a monogamous marriage of every single thing to a single region of space-time, rests on nothing but dogma. It is at least worth exploring theories which rest on a contrary, more permissive attitude to spatio-temporal location.

So, suppose that we try to preserve both the principle of One Over Many, and its close modal cousin, the principle of Robustness. This enables us to capture the manifest facts of recurrence adequately. When Albina and Bianca both have whiteness, there is something they both have (One Over Many); and Albina *could still* have had the very same colour, even if Bianca had not (Robustness—a kind of One Over Many Possible-Situations).

This sort of theory can be called a *Platonic* theory of universals, in honour of Plato, who seems to have held views of this general character.

If we take such a view, we will have to abandon the principle of Sufficiency; the things which satisfy One Over Many and Robustness cannot serve as adequate truthmakers. The lesson to learn from the Fox paradox is that universals have no privileged status with respect to truths.

Good historical precedents can be given for applying the term 'universals' to those things which supply truthmakers for truths—to *whatever* there is, *in addition to* individuals, in virtue of which these individuals are the ways they are, in virtue of which various things are true of them. If we were to use the term 'universals' for truthmakers, then the sorts of things which satisfy a Robust One Over Many would not be 'universals'.

And yet what is in a name? I will not defend my choice of terminology, but just explain it. When I speak of universals, when I say mathematics is the theory of universals, I do *not* mean to be speaking of the sorts of things which generate truths from individuals. What *I* mean by 'universals' are things which can be wholly present in many separate regions at the same time, and which could still have been present in some of those regions even if they had not been present in others.

The things I call universals, then, fall short of satisfying Sufficiency. The failure of Sufficiency in Platonic theories generates justified uneasiness. Think about it: for instance Bianca and whiteness both exist in the Actual World, where B is true, where Bianca *has* whiteness; yet they also exist in the Other world, where B is false. Since B is true in the one world and false in the other, surely even a Platonist would like to be able to say that there must be something which is in just one of these worlds, and which *makes* it different from the other world.

Thus it is tempting for a Platonist to say that there must be something extra, call it ε, which exists in the Actual World but is absent in the Other World, and which makes the difference, making B true in the first case and false in the second. For instance it is tempting to say that, for it to be true that Bianca has whiteness, it must be true not only that Bianca exists, and that whiteness exists, but also that there be some *relationship* between Bianca and whiteness—that Bianca should 'instantiate' whiteness.

Yet this way of stating the matter misconstrues the manner in which the Fox paradox was constructed. I set down β to be *whatever* thing or *things* were required, together with b, to get a complete truthmaker, entailing the truth of B. If ε is one of the things required, then it is *already* one of the things included in β. So there is no way its 'introduction' could solve our problems.

If a Platonist introduces ε, in an attempt to satisfy Sufficiency, this is very likely to lead to an infinite regress. One is reminded of Aristotle's so-called third-man argument against Platonic theories; or of Bradley's so-called relation-regress. If ε is treated as a Robust One Over Many, then its existence, in turn, will *still* be insufficient to entail the truth of B. So we will need a further relationship to link ε with Bianca and whiteness. Platonists with the stomach for it may be willing to swallow such an infinite regress, just as set theorists have swallowed the burgeoning hierarchy of sets of sets. Perhaps the situation of Bianca's having whiteness simply does contain infinitely many constituents, in somewhat the way that a line contains infinitely many parts. And yet—whether the regress is vicious or benign—this whole issue is beside the point for the Fox paradox. I constructed the paradox in such a way as to cut across these issues by specifying that β was to include *everything* we need to generate a complete truthmaker.

If an infinite hierarchy of instantiation relations were needed to complete a truthmaker for B, then that whole infinite hierarchy must be stuffed into β. And the Fox paradox will still go through unaffected. The Third Man is not the Fox.

Nevertheless, I was persuaded by Denis Robinson that it is worth exploring theories which involve what I call *Robinson's merger*, theories which contain both a component which meets Sufficiency, and also a component which supplies a Robust One Over Many. The trick is to use two different entities for the two different jobs.

A Platonist cannot *add* any ε to α or β to satisfy Sufficiency; any ε which worked would have to have been in α or β already. Yet suppose a Platonist were investigating a property-instance theory which seems to work. In that theory $\alpha \neq \beta$. Suppose the Platonist grants this.

But then a Platonist begins to pry into the constituents of α and β. And they claim to find that α contains two constituents,

α^- and δ

and likewise β contains two constituents,

β^- and δ.

The theory we are examining is a theory of truthmakers; so by the Fox paradox we must stick to $\alpha \neq \beta$. Hence $\alpha^- \neq \beta^-$. That will be enough to enable us to meet Sufficiency without landing in the Fox contradiction. Nevertheless, the Platonist claims, there is a single thing, a One Over Many, δ, which occurs among the truthmakers for A *and* among the truthmakers for B. A Platonist may urge that this is sufficient to vindicate their Platonism. And I agree.

An anti-Platonist might wish to resist the decomposition of α into $(\alpha^- + \delta)$ and β into $(\beta^- + \delta)$. Yet an anti-Platonist cannot always resist such decompositions. Let A be the truth that I see the moon. The existence of me, a, is necessary but not sufficient for the truth of A; so there must be some other thing or things α whose existence together with me entails the truth of A. Similarly, let B be the truth that you see the moon; and this truth requires the existence of you, b, together with some further thing or things, β. To satisfy Sufficiency we must have $\alpha \neq \beta$; but no plausible property-instance theory will be able to deny that

$\alpha = x +$ the moon,
$\beta = y +$ the moon,

for some x and y. If a further attempt is made to decompose x and y to reveal a common element, then there is no reason *in principle* why a property-instance theorist should not allow it. What we must insist, however, is that if we want to meet Sufficiency, then no matter how often a common element is extracted, we must always have $\alpha \neq \beta$, and so what remains of α cannot be identical with what remains of β. There must always be a non-recurrence, property-instance residue.

So the uncovering of an overlap between the truthmakers for A and B should cause no embarrassment for a property-instance theorist. Nor need it be any triumph for the Platonist—so far. After all, the moon may well be granted as among the truthmakers for truths about you, and about me, but the moon is not a One Over Many in the required sense.

Yet all that Platonists need to add, to vindicate their Platonism, is that at least sometimes the relevant decomposition will yield a common constituent, δ, which is a universal in the recurrence sense—something which hangs loose over space-time. There is nothing in a property-instance account of truthmakers which rules out the existence of universals in that sense.

There is thus no obvious barrier to Robinson's merger. One can believe in both truthmakers and recurrence-universals as long as you remember that the universals are not the truthmakers, and the truthmakers are not universals.

What emerges is a theory on which, for at least some truths, like A, there will be several things required to constitute a complete truthmaker: some individual, a, some universal, δ, and something else, α^-. What should we conceive this something else, α^-, to be?

We could think of α^- as a kind of property-instance, or rather, a relation-instance, say, as the 'having of δ by a'. This particular instantiation-instance could not have existed if A had not been true, so its existence entails that A. Hence it will be an adequate truthmaker for A. Similarly, β^-, 'b's having δ', will be a truthmaker for B.

Calling α^- and β^- 'instantiation-instances' suggests a conception on which they are like little dabs of glue which stick δ first to Albina and then to Bianca. But there is another conception we could have of them; and this other conception is suggested by redescribing the situation in slightly different terminology. Notice that the existence of α^- entails the truth of A, and hence entails the existence of both Albina and δ. Think of α^- as *entailing* the existence of Albina and δ, by way of *containing* both Albina and δ as parts.

Under this conception, α^- becomes a fact, or situation, or state of affairs. The entity α^- is the fact of 'Albina's having δ'; similarly, β^- is the fact of 'Bianca's having δ'.

Facts, however, are puzzling sorts of entities. I take them to be entities which *contain* particulars and universals as *constituents*. Thus for instance the fact of 'Albina's having δ' will contain both the particular Albina, and the universal, δ, as constituents. The question we must then ask is whether we can construe this fact as *merely* the aggregate of Albina and δ. Or we do need to allow that the fact contains some third constituent?

Suppose the fact is construed as having some such third constituent. Then this third constituent will more or less inevitably turn out to be an analogue of a property-instance—'the having of δ by Albina'. Such a theory of facts, then, will be a variant of the theory of property-instances discussed earlier. It offers no new solution to the Fox paradox; it merely points out ways in which the old property-instance theory could be fleshed out if we were to supplement it with a theory of aggregates.

Yet it may be worth seeing whether a theory of facts could be constructed which was not merely a variant of a theory of property-instances.

24 States of Affairs

Suppose that the fact of 'Albina's having δ' were construed as simply the aggregate of Albina and δ; and, similarly, suppose the fact of 'Bianca's having δ' were construed as simply the aggregate of Bianca and δ. Call this the Simple aggregate theory of facts, or states of affairs.

On this theory, the truthmaker for A, which I have been calling α^-, will be the aggregate of Albina and δ. It will be best, in such a theory, to rename α^- as, say, S(A). Similarly, the truthmaker for B, β^-, will be the aggregate of Bianca and δ, and will be renamed S(B). In the Actual World, where A and B are both true, both S(A) and S(B) exist; in the Other World, A is true but B is false, and so S(A) exists but S(B) doesn't.

For some time, I thought that this suggestion could be met by a quick refutation, as follows. Consider the Actual World, where A is true and B is true, the aggregate of Albina and δ exists, and the aggregate of Bianca and δ exists. The existence of the aggregate of Bianca and δ is being proposed as the truthmaker for B. Hence the existence of this aggregate must *entail* the truth of B. Yet consider the Other World, where B is false even though Bianca still exists. In this Other World, A is true, and its truthmaker is the aggregate of Albina and δ. Hence δ exists in the Other World. So both Bianca and δ exist in the Other World. Therefore the aggregate of Bianca and δ exists in the Other World. And from this it would follow that B is true in the Other World, contrary to our stipulative definition of this Other World. Thus the assumption that the truthmaker for B is merely the aggregate of Bianca and δ leads to a contradiction.

Discussion with Mark Johnston and David Lewis at Princeton has convinced me that this argument is too swift. It may be rescuable, but it rests on a key assumption which must be more clearly acknowledged and laid open to debate. This debatable assumption can be drawn out as follows.

In arguing against the Simple aggregate theory, I have assumed that since Bianca and δ exist in the Other World, therefore 'the aggregate of Bianca and δ' exists in the Other World. But this assumption can be broken into several parts: (1) There exists something in the Other World which is *an* aggregate of Bianca and δ. (2) There exists something, S(B), in the Actual World which is *an* aggregate of Bianca and δ. (3) The aggregate of Bianca and δ in the Actual World is numerically identical with the aggregate of Bianca and δ in the Other World.

(In the framework of a counterpart theory, the point will be put differently, but will have the same resultant force. In such a framework, my argument against the Simple aggregate theory will rest in the assumption that:

> *The counterpart of an aggregate will always by the aggregate of the counterparts of its constituents.*

Thus, for instance, a counterpart-theoretic argument against the Simple aggregate theory would have to assume the following. In the Actual World, we have individual b and universal δ. In the Other World, we have individual d and universal δ. Suppose the very same universal δ is found in both worlds; and that d is the counterpart of b. Then the argument I outlined against the Simple aggregate theory assumes that the aggregate of d and δ will be the counterpart of the aggregate of b and δ, since d is the counterpart of b. This assumption will then be the counterpart-theoretic counterpart of my assumption that the aggregate of b and δ in the Actual World is numerically identical with the aggregate of b and δ in the Other World.)

My argument against the Simple aggregate theory thus rests on an assumption about the essences of aggregates. It rests on the assumption that if something is an aggregate of certain parts, then that *same* something would exist, and contain just those parts, in any possible situation in which those parts exist.

Yet this is implausible. Consider the ship of Theseus, made from a thousand planks. Plausibly, the ship is an aggregate, containing all the planks as parts, and containing nothing else. And yet, if the planks had remained in the warehouse, and no one had put them together to make a ship, then *the ship* would not have existed. There would have been something else instead, a stack of planks perhaps. And that too would have been an aggregate containing all the planks as parts, and nothing else. But the aggregate which is the actual *ship* is not the same thing as the aggregate which would have been just a *stack*.

In reflecting on the case of the ship, you may be led to wonder whether a ship *is*, after all, just an aggregate containing all the planks as parts, and containing nothing else. Following this drift of thought, however, will lead us back to the sort of theory which turns out to be a variant of the theory of property-instances. That may be all very well, but it is tangential to my current concern.

I want to explore the possibility of a theory which treats a fact as just an aggregate of particulars and universals. If we are to explore that possibility, we should cling on to the intuition that a ship is an aggregate of planks. We may be tempted to add that it is an aggregate of planks *and universals*. But if these universals are to be a genuine One Over Many, then they too could still have existed even if that ship had not instantiated them. From the perspective of the overall structure of the argument, such universals may be thought of as merely extra planks. And so the point will remain, that if the ship *is* an aggregate of any such sort (not including property-instances), then such an aggregate may fail to exist *even if* its parts were all to exist.

Let us take stock, then, of what a theory of states of affairs would be like if it were to amount to something other than icing on the cake for a theory of property-instances.

The truthmaker for a truth, such as that Bianca has whiteness, will be an aggregate of particulars and universals, such as the aggregate of Bianca and whiteness. If Bianca has not had whiteness, then this aggregate would not have existed. Both Bianca and whiteness might still have existed, so *an* aggregate could have existed which contained Bianca and whiteness. But that aggregate would have been a different thing from the aggregate which actually exists. Why would that aggregate have been a diferent thing? Presumably because Bianca would not have *had* whiteness. The aggregate would not have been an appropriate sort of 'complex unity' (Russell's term (1912)); its constituents would not have been 'together' (Goodman's term (1951)). For the fact S(B) to exist, then, the fact of Bianca's having whiteness, we require not only that its constituents exist, but also that they meet some further condition. But the satisfaction of this further condition cannot be construed in terms of the existence of some further constituent in the fact. The fact S(B) contains b and δ, Bianca and whiteness, and nothing else. But if Bianca had not had whiteness, then S(B) would not have existed.

The resulting theory has certain merits. It satisfies Truthmaker. And it makes room for universals which constitute a genuine One Over Many. And yet it is intuitively unsatisfying. It is unsatisfying because it allows two aggregates to be numerically distinct *without any difference in their constituents*. And this runs counter to the spirit of the Truthmaker axiom. The space which Truthmaker tries to bridge between objects and facts has been relocated rather than bridged. It re-emerges as a gap between a thing and its constituents. Truthmaker forbids any difference in truth without a difference in what exists. But we are now permitting something analogous—that there could be distinctions between things without any difference in their parts.

Truthmaker can, indeed, be seen as a special case of an axiom governing aggregates:

There can be no difference in wholes without a difference in parts.

Consider two possible worlds. For them to be distinct, there must be something true in one which is false in the other. But regard them as wholes, built up from parts. Then, for them to be distinct, there must be something which is part of one but not part of the other. The need for truthmakers thus emerges as merely an aspect of the need for a difference in parts when there is a difference in wholes.

I conclude that the theory that truthmakers are facts must either merge with a theory of property-instances, or else it will satisfy Truthmaker in letter only, and not in spirit.

And even if a theory of facts is accepted, the deeper point remains: that *universals* must not be construed as *truthmakers*.

25   Categories of Being

THE inescapable outcome of the Fox paradox is that the things which satisfy a robust principle of One Over Many will not be things which satisfy Sufficiency. That is to say, recurrence-universals will not be things whose existence entails the various truths concerning their instantiations.

Truthmaker can be satisfied, not by universls, but by either states of affairs, or property-instances. And under scrutiny these two options boil down to much the same thing. The difference between property-instances and states of affairs is little more than a difference in visualizations and metaphors.

Property-instances, however, do not serve as a comfortable subject-matter for mathematics, at least at first blush. Some might argue that despite appearances, mathematics might be construed as a theory of property-instances, or more particularly a theory of sets of property-instances. I do not claim to have refuted that view. I am concerned only to explore one theory of mathematics, not to refute all others; and the theory I am exploring is one which takes mathematics to be a theory of universals. For my purposes, property-instances are of interest only as illustrating one way in which you might satisfy Truthmaker *without* universals.

Can you satisfy Truthmaker *with* universals? Yes; by a theory of states of affairs. Truthmakers are identified with states of affairs, and states of affairs contain universals as constituents. Yet, in such a theory, although universals are constituents in truthmakers, so are individuals. And there is nothing distinctive about the role which universals play as far as truthmaking is concerned. But states of affairs do not constitute the subject-matter of mathematics.

So far, then, what Truthmaker motivates are not the sorts of things we need to furnish the subject-matter of mathematics. Yet there is one more child of Truthmaker which needs to be scrutinized; perhaps it might serve as a foundation for mathematics.

One response one can take is to cling onto the Truthmaker axiom and abandon recurrence-universals. This is the course taken by theories of property-instances. But the contrary strategy is worth exploring as well: the strategy of abandoning the Truthmaker axiom.

And yet there is something very unsatisfying about a blank denial of Truthmaker. For this reason, it is worth seeing whether we can *replace* Truthmaker by some other principle which captures the irrepressible and manifest truth behind Truthmaker, and yet which alters the principle enough to permit us to escape from the Fox paradox.

Compare two possible situations. In one of these situations we have a particular, a say, and a truth about that particular, A say. In the other possible situation, although the same particular a still exists, nevertheless the truth A no longer holds of it.

There is then a deep conviction which voices itself as the claim that *there must be* something which makes the one situation different from the other. This at least appears to be an existential claim. Taken at face value, it asserts the *existence* of something—the existence of some *thing*—a thing whose existence makes the one situation different from the other.

Yet there is an intriguing alternative way of trying to voice the deep conviction that there is something which makes the situations different. This alternative draws upon what is called *second-order quantification*.

Consider the following attempt to re-articulate the conviction behind Truthmaker:

> In order for something to be true, there must not only be certain individual things, but *there must also be somehow* that these things are.

The first 'there must . . . be' is a *first-order* quantifier. The second 'there must . . . be' is a *second-order* quantifier. It is to be taken just as seriously as the first-order quantifier, and is not to be passed away as a mere manner of speaking. It is to be taken as having, in some sense, as much ontological force as the first-order quantifier. And yet the second-order quantifier is to be regarded as different, somehow, from the first-order one. The two kinds of quantification should not be conflated, or such, at least, is the suggestion I now wish to explore.

On this view, the claim that there is somehow that certain things are should not commit us to saying that there is some further *thing* which *is* this 'somehow' that they are. The second-order 'there is somehow . . .' does not entail the first-order 'there is something . . .'.

In mathematical terms this amounts to a separation of a fundamental sort between *functions* and *objects*. It is standardly assumed in mathematics that whenever there is a function mapping objects of one sort onto objects of a second sort, then we can also study an object of a third sort: the set of ordered pairs whose first member is an object of the first sort, and whose second member is the corresponding object of the second sort. In fact, the relevant 'function' is standardly *identified* with that corresponding set of ordered pairs. The view I now wish to explore is one which resists this sort of identification; it is a view according to which there is a fundamental difference between the 'being' of a function relating two objects and the 'being' of an object (a set of ordered pairs for instance) containing those objects. On this view, *a function is not a set of ordered pairs.*

In trying to articulate a theory of this sort, it is very hard to keep matters clear when using a natural language like English. There is a strong impulse to display what one is getting at by using the symbolic notation of formal logic. I will yield to that impulse.

The idea behind second-order quantification is that when a simple predication like

   F*a*

is true, then we can infer that there is something which is F:

   $\exists x.Fx$;

but we can also infer that there is somehow that the individual *a* is:

   $\exists \phi.\phi a.$

Consider now a statement,

   (F*a* & F*b*)

which predicates 'the same thing' of *a* and *b*. In such a case we would like to say that *a* and *b* 'have something in common'. In a first-order articulation of this idea, we would have to say that there is something (other than *a* and *b*), and which *is* the thing which *a* and *b* have in common,

   $\exists x. (\text{has } (a,x) \ \& \ \text{has } (b,x))$.

But using second-order logic, we can formulate things differently. We can say instead that there is somehow that *a* is and *b* is:

   $\exists \phi.(\phi a \ \& \ \phi b)$

—'there is somehow that *a* is, and *b* is that-how too'. Notice that this not only seems to capture the truth behind the Truthmaker, it also captures something of the spirit of One Over Many.

What is crucial here is that the quantifier ' $\exists \phi$' binds symbols which take the position of a predicate, like the 'F' in 'Fa'; it cannot bind a symbol which is a name of some thing, like the 'a' in 'Fa'. There is a deep distinction to be drawn between one sort of 'there is' and the other. The sort of 'thing there is' when *there is somehow* that something is, can never be the sort of 'thing there is' when *there is something* that is somehow. The quantifiers are of different 'logical types'. A theory built on them is called a *type theory*. It is often characterized by saying that individuals constitute a different category of being from properties and relations—both are said to be, or to exist, but they 'exist' in quite different senses.

Natural languages have a seemingly indomitable drive to 'nominalize' the expression of a type theory. In place of

$\exists \phi.(\phi a \ \& \ \phi b)$

it is tempting to say something like:

There is some *property* a has and b has, or
some *concept* a and b both fall under.

And this begs to be misconstrued as

$\exists x.(\text{Property}(x) \ \& \ \text{has} \ (a,x) \ \& \ \text{has} \ (b,x))$, or
$\exists x.(\text{Concept}(x) \ \& \ \text{falls under} \ (a,x) \ \& \ \text{falls under} \ (b,x))$.

The impulse to thus misconstrue second-order quantification is aggravated by current orthodoxy in semantics and model theory. When setting out to describe the semantics of second-order logic, we naturally turn to the sorts of techniques exemplified in Tarski's celebrated theory of truth. We begin with a *set* of objects, called a domain; and to any individual constant, like a, we assign a *member* of the domain; and individual variables, like x, are taken to range over all the objects in the domain. To each predicate constant, like F, we assign a *subset* of the domain; and predicate variables, like ϕ, are taken to range over all subsets of the domain.

Under this sort of semantics, second-order predication becomes just an alternative notation for set theory. The claim that 'there is somehow that a is'

$\exists \phi.\phi a$

becomes merely an alternative way of saying that 'there is some set of which a is a member':

$\exists x.(a \varepsilon x)$;

or more cautiously, 'there is some subset of the domain of which a is a member'.

Yet there are reasons for doubting whether such semantics capture adequately the intended interpretation of second-order quantifications. George Boolos (1975, 1984) has explored some of the intriguing reasons why standard semantics may be misconstruing second-order quantification.

Consider for instance the following assertion:

$$\exists \phi \forall x.\phi x.$$

This says that there is somehow that everything is. This is a true assertion of second-order quantification theory (indeed it is a *valid* assertion, that is it is true under *all* standard interpretations). There is indeed somehow that everything is: self-identical, for instance. We may generalize on any given truth

$$a = a$$

to obtain

$$\forall x.(x = x);$$

and this entails

$$\exists \phi \forall x.\phi x.$$

But suppose we interpret predicates by assigning to them various sets. And suppose we take an assertion like

$$\exists \phi.\phi a$$

to be an alternative notation for the set-theoretical assertion that there is some set to which a belongs:

$$\exists y.a\varepsilon y.$$

Under this construal, the formula

$$\exists \phi \forall x.\phi x$$

would *seem* to assert that *there is some set to which everything belongs*.

And yet Cantor showed us that there can be no set to which everything belongs. For each set there will be subsets of this set; and not all of these subsets can also be members of the given set. Hence not everything can be a member of the given set. And thus there can be no set which contains everything.

How then can the formula ' $\exists \phi \forall x.\phi x$' be true, even though it *seems* to say there is some set to which everything belongs? The orthodox answer is this. In order for the formula to be either true or false, it must first be interpreted. In order to interpret it, we must choose some set as a domain. Under any given interpretation, based on a given domain, the sentence ' ∃ φ ∀ x.φx' comes out as true because there is a set which everything *in the domain* belongs to, for instance the domain itself.

Yet this is not faithful to the spirit of the second-order claim 'There is somehow that everything is.' We want such a claim to be true even when the quantifiers range over *everything*, not just over everything in some chosen domain.

There are contexts in which we intend our quantifiers to range over *everything there is*. (Note that I use 'there are' in saying this!) Perhaps our intentions here are inconsistent. But perhaps the trouble lies not in our intention, but rather, in our attempt to articulate that intention within a *first-order* semantic theory.

To take second-order quantification seriously, on its own terms, we must approach its semantics in a manner analogous to the treatment we give to first-order quantifiers, construed—as we say—*objectually*. Let me explain.

By calling a first-order quantifier an 'objectual' one, or by construing it thus, we distinguish it from what is called a *substitutional* quantifier. Suppose a formula

$$\exists\, x.Fx$$

contains a quantifier-symbol, ' ∃ ', which is to be interpreted in such a way that the given formula is taken to be true if and only if *there is some name*, a, such that

$$Fa$$

is a true formula. That is the sentence '∃ x.Fx' is to be true just when it has some true *substitution-instance*, like 'Fa'. In this case ' ∃ ' is said to be a substitutional quantifier.

Objectual quantification is different. An objectual quantifier ' ∃ ' will be such that the formula

$$\exists\, x.Fx$$

will be true just when there is something—*whether or not it has a name*—such that it is an F. Thus for instance the sentence 'There are unnamed roses' is true when objectually construed; but it cannot be true when substitutionally construed.

Now look closely at how our metalanguage describes the semantics of the objectual quantifier. We find that we must *use* an objectual quantifier in the metalanguage when giving the semantics for the object-language, as we do for instance by saying:

'∃ x.Fx' is true iff *there is something* which is an F.

By taking second-order quantification seriously, I mean the insistence on an analogous replication of the object-language sort of quantifier within the metalanguage. Thus, for instance, our semantic theory will take second-order quantification seriously if it says things like:

'∃ φ.φa' is true iff *there is somehow* that a is.

Theories of second-order predication and quantification are, I fear, in a misty state, philosophically speaking. They echo some aspects of Aristotle's writings on universals. But the greatest landmark in the history of second-order quantification was the work of Gottlob Frege, for instance in his *Grundgesetze*. I take it that Frege's insistence on a deep and uncrossable gulf between *objects* and *concepts* was a heroic attempt to take second-order quantification seriously.

There is, however, an unfortunate feature of Frege's exposition which keeps sucking us back down into first-order, ersatz versions of the sort of theory he was aiming for. The word 'concepts' is not appropriate for the purposes it is intended for, since it fits into the linguistic slot where *names* go. The words 'properties, or 'universals', or 'sets', or Whitehead and Russell's 'propositional functions' are all just as bad.

Seriously second-order theories must forbear from ever equating second-order claims, about 'somehow that things are', to *any* first-order claims that *there are* some further entities, however called, and however 'fundamentally different' they are said to be from 'individuals'. There is somehow that things are, but there can be nothing which is identical to this 'somehow'. As Frege said, properly speaking, *identity* does not apply to *concepts* (for a very explicit statement of this, see for instance his *Posthumous Writings* (1979, p. 120), a passage from which I will be quoting at greater length later). But the word 'concepts' may lead us astray here. The real point is that a sentence of the form:

∃φ(. . . φ . . .)

(There is somehow such that . . .)

is *not* equivalent to any statement of the form

∃x. (. . . x . . .)

(There is something such that . . .).

And so for instance

$$\exists \phi.(\phi a \ \& \ \phi b)$$

will *not* be equivalent to *anything* of the form

$$\exists x.(Cx \ \& \ R(x,a) \ \& \ R(x,b)),$$

where 'C' is any predicate (such as 'is a concept', 'is a property', 'is a universal', 'is a set', or whatever), and where 'R' is any relational predicate (such as 'is true of', 'applies to', 'is had by', 'is instantiated by', 'contains as a member', or whatever).

If Frege and Boolos are right, and we do need second-order quantification, then this evacuates most of the motivation for theories of property-instances or states of affairs. We no longer need them in order to supply truthmakers: we can supply truthmakers by appeal to individuals and recurrence-universals, plus second-order quantification. So we need not introduce any such putative truthmakers as property-instances or states of affairs.

Or perhaps we could say that second-order quantification serves to *analyse* rather than to eliminate states of affairs. We can say that an aggregate of a particular and a universal counts as a 'state of affairs' provided there is *somehow* that the particular stands to the universal, namely it instantiates that universal. Instantiation serves to 'complete' a truthmaker, a state of affairs, but its 'existence' is irreducibly second-order; it cannot be construed as a universal.

The idea of taking second-order quantification seriously stands in need of much clarification. Yet because it holds out the hope of generating a better theory of universals, it is worth pursuing it a little way even in the absence of much needed clarification. Second-order quantification seems to enable us to capture the spirit of both Truthmaker, *and* Recurrence. So it might offer a distinctive way of resolving the Fox paradox, and of providing a subject-matter for mathematics.

26   The Second-order Fox

THE Fox paradox is an inconsistent tetrad. The mere existence of second-order quantification does not render this tetrad consistent. If we are to use second-order quantifiers to resolve the paradox, then we must use them to *reformulate* the four principles in this inconsistent tetrad.

Initially, it is hard to see how second-order quantifiers could possibly render the Fox tetrad consistent. In presenting the paradox, I used roman letters a, b, c, d, to represent individuals; the Greek letters α, β, γ, to represent the extra 'whatevers' which are needed to fill out adequate truthmakers for the relevant truths. So I am already well on the way towards observing the sort of syntactic distinctions, the sort of gulf between categories of being, which type theories make so crucial. How then can a type theory block the derivation of a contradiction? In the end, I will argue that it can't. But first let us examine more closely the way the Fox paradox will look from the perspective of second-order quantification.

The first thing to explore is the question: What happens to the principle of Sufficiency under second-order logic? The principle of Sufficiency, we may remember, requires that there should *be* certain things whose existence entails the relevant truth. So this is clearly a principle which will be deeply affected by a doctrine of *categories of being*.

Sufficiency requires, for instance, that when A is true, *there must be* some thing or things whose existence entails that it is true. But now 'existence' has bifurcated into two senses. We need therefore to look at how these two senses are to be construed; and in particular we need to find a way of construing the two senses in terms of the two sorts of quantifier—first-order and second-order.

A first-order claim that something, *a* say, exists, is standardly captured by:

$$\exists x(x = a)$$

—'There is something which is *a*.' Existence is explained by using a *quantifier* plus *identity*.

Presumably second-order existence claims should be formulated analogously in order to link them analogously with second-order quantification. So consider the suggestion that second-order existence claims should be construed as having something like the following form:

$\exists \phi.(F \doteq \phi)$,

('there is somehow which being F is'),

where '$\doteq$' is to be some second-order counterpart of the first-order relation of existence. The symbol '$\doteq$' cannot be the identity sign itself, '$=$'; not, at any rate, if second-order quantification is to be taken seriously in the manner of a theory of logical types. So we need some account of the nature of the second-order identity relation, $\doteq$, and presumably this second-order relation will need to be modelled on the first-order relation.

The standard account of first-order identity is given by Leibniz's law: that an individual is numerically distinct from another individual if and only if something is true of the one which is not true of the other:

$(x = y)$ if and only if
$\forall \phi.(\phi x$ iff $\phi y)$.

There are two ways of modelling second-order identity on Leibnizian first-order identity. One way is clearly outlined in Frege (1979, p. 120).

And in the same way the relation of equality, by which I understand complete coincidence, identity, can only be thought of as holding for objects, not concepts . . . But although the relation of equality can only be thought of as holding for objects, there is an analogous relation for concepts, since this is a relation between concepts I call it a second level relation, whereas the former relation I call a first level relation. We say that an object a is equal to an object b (in the sense of coinciding with it) if a falls under every concept under which b falls, and conversely. We obtain something corresponding to this for concepts if we switch the roles of concept and object. We could then say that the relation we had in mind above holds between the concept Φ and the concept X, if every object that falls under Φ also falls under X, and conversely.

In other words, we can define a second-level relation which I will call *identity from below*, $\eqcirc$, thus:

$(F \eqcirc G)$ if and only if
$\forall x.(Fx$ iff $Gx)$.

I borrow the term 'identity from below', and the symbol '$\eqcirc$' from Dana Scott, 'More on the Axiom of Extensionality' (see Bar Hillel *et al.*, 1962).

Now compare Frege's strategy with an alternative way of modelling second-order identity on Leibniz's law. Instead of 'switching the roles' of concept and object in Leibniz's law, we could define a different sort of second-order identity by 'boosting' the whole Leibnizian definition up a level. We could say that two concepts are *identical from above* when everything which is true of one is true of the other:

$(F \doteq G)$ if and only if
$\forall \ \Phi.(\Phi F \ \text{iff} \ \Phi G)$,

where Φ is a 'third-order' variable—ranging over properties of properties—and where it is replaceable by any sentence fragment which can be turned into a completed sentence by the insertion of a predicate or open sentence.

This definition of 'identity from above' is close to the definition used by Whitehead and Russell in the first edition of their *Principia Mathematica*.

It seems to me that 'boosting' Leibniz's law, to obtain 'identity from above', is somewhat more natural and obvious than Frege's procedure of 'switching the roles' of concept and object. So I would like to be given some good reason for construing second-order identity Frege's way. Given Frege's own advocacy of higher-order logic, including third-order quantification, his insistence on what I call identity from below is undermotivated, at least by what he says.

In contrast, when Quine uses a similar strategy for defining identity from below, it has a sharper bite, given Quine's commitment to the view that so-called higher-order quantification is at best merely an obfuscating alternative notation for a theory of classes. (See for instance Quine (1953, Ch. 6.) If all truths, (ΦF), involving a predicate F were really just truths of first-order quantification theory, as Quine urges, then identity from above would simply collapse into identity from below. But since I am here exploring the outcome of taking second-order quantification seriously, it is not to be simply *presupposed* that all higher-order truths collapse into first-order truths. So Frege needs some defence of his preference for identity from below.

A clear challenge to the collapse urged by Quine comes from *modal* truths, truths not just about how individual things are, but about how they could have been. Thus, for instance, suppose that everything which is this-how is also that-how, and vice versa:

$\forall \ x.(Fx \ \text{iff} \ Gx)$,

and so

(F = G);

and we thus have a case of identity from below. But suppose that it would be possible for something to be this-how but not that-how:

Possibly ($\exists$ x.(Fx & not-Gx)).

Treat this as 'something which is true of F':

'ΦF' abbreviates
'Possibly. ($\exists$ x.(Fx & not-Gx))';

we can read 'ΦF' as saying 'F is such that *possibly it is had by something which is not G*'.

This is something which is true of F, but *not* true of G: it is *not* true of G that 'possibly it is had by something which is not G':

Not-Possibly. ($\exists$ x.(Gx & not-Gx)),

that is,

Not Φ G.

Hence it is true that ΦF but not true that ΦG; and so it is *not* the case that everything true of F is true of G and vice versa. That is

Not $\forall$ Φ. (ΦF iff ΦG);

and therefore

Not (F = G),

that is F and G are identical from below, but they are not identical from above.

If the only truths involving predicates were those of modal predicate logic, then second-order *identity from above* would amount to *necessary coextensiveness*. Yet if there are still further truths, beyond those formulable in modal predicate logic, then identity from above may well individuate much more finely than necessary coextensiveness. Indeed, if we consider truths about what people *think*, what they *say*, and what they *mean*, then it can be argued that, as long as two predicates are non-synonymous, there will *always* be truths featuring one predicate which cease to be true when replaced by the other. And hence two non-synonymous predicates will always represent second-order beings which are not identical from above. The claim (F = G) will be true *only* if 'F' and 'G' are synonymous. Or so it would seem.

I leave it an open question how finely identity from above will discriminate among predicates. I will return, rather, to the problem of reformulating the principle of Sufficiency in a second-order framework.

The principle of Sufficiency required that when A or B are true, *there must be* things which make them true; thus we asserted:

Sufficiency
The existence of a and α entail that A;
. . . etc.

But we now need to reassess what an attribution of 'existence' to α will amount to, construed in a second-order manner. Let us use second-order identity to attempt this reassessment. I will appeal only to identity from above, since this is the more sophisticated notion, and can be simply adjusted or supplemented to subsume identity from below as a special case.

Let us take a to be an individual, but 'α' to be a second-order symbol, or predicate. Existence for an individual like a is naturally attributed by

$$\exists x.(x = a);$$

and the natural analogue for a second-order being like α would be:

$$\exists \Phi.(\Phi \doteq \alpha).$$

The trouble with these construals of these existence-claims, is that they fail to make Sufficiency come out true. The second-order attribution of existence to a and α will *not* entail *that a is an α*; it will not entail A.

To enable second-order existence to be of any help to us in satisfying Truthmaker or Sufficiency, we must evidently reconstrue it by including an Aristotelian requirement that for a property to *exist*; it must be *had* by something. So, suppose we reconstrue a second-order existence claim, 'α exists', as something like:

$$\exists \phi.((\phi \doteq \alpha) \ \& \ \exists x.(\phi x)).$$

Now let us see what happens to the principle of Sufficiency under such a construal. Sufficiency requires that:

The existence of a and α entails that A.

Suppose first that α satisfies One Over Many—it is the same somehow that both Albina and Bianca are when they both have whiteness. Under this supposition, the existence of Albina, a, together with there being such a somehow as α, does *not* entail that Albina has whiteness. Albina could well exist with some other colour; and yet there could still *be* the same somehow that Albina *was*, and indeed someone else, like Bianca, may still be that same somehow.

Thus, an α which satisfies One Over Many cannot satisfy Sufficiency, even when construed in a second-order manner, and requiring instantiations for all second-order 'existents'.

Suppose however, in contrast, that we were to take α to be something more like a second-order incarnation of a *property-instance*. Suppose α to be: 'has whiteness *and* is identical to Albina'. If this exists, in the Aristotelian second-order sense, then it *does* follow necessarily that A is true, that Albina has whiteness. But the second-order existence of *this* α does not entail the truth of B. So the truthmaker for B must be a β which is not identical with α: β must be 'has whiteness and is identical to Bianca'; and not ($\alpha \doteq \beta$). So we can satisfy Sufficiency, but the cost has been a violation of One Over Many.

We could also try raising the Taylor twist up to a second-order framework; that is we could try taking both α and β to be the same second-order reincarnation of an *aggregate* of property-instances. Consider a *relation* which holds between two things just when one is Albina, the other is Bianca, and both have whiteness. And let α and β both be identified with this same relation. Such a relation will be expressible by an open sentence with two free variables, x and y:

(x has whiteness & y has whiteness & x = a & y = b),

which we may abbreviate as:

$S(x, y)$.

To identify α and β with this relation, is to set

$\alpha \doteq \beta \doteq S$.

Given the second-order *existence* of this relation, construed as requiring instantiation, we can indeed infer from the existence of α or β to the truth of A and B. That is the 'Aristotelian-existence' of this α or β *does* entail that Albina has whiteness and that Bianca has whiteness. So we satisfy Sufficiency, and have a truthmaker for A and B. We also satisfy One Over Many, $\alpha \doteq \beta$.

And yet Robustness fails! We do not have that $\alpha \doteq \gamma$. In the Other World, where Bianca does not have whiteness, the truthmaker for A is the existence of Albina together with γ. So whatever γ is, it has to exist in the Other World, and its existence there must entail that Albina has whiteness; yet α, in contrast, does *not* exist in the Other World—in the appropriate sense of existence. The reason α does not exist in the Other World is that in that world Bianca does not have whiteness. This entails that the relation $S(x, y)$ is not instantiated in that world. And β has been identified with just that relation; so β does not exist in the Other World. And hence γ, the truthmaker for A in the Other World, cannot be α.

The Fox paradox thus stands, even when boosted into a second-order framework. We cannot satisfy all four members of the inconsistent Fox tetrad. A second-order theory merely replicates precisely the pattern generated by property-instance theories. We can satisfy Sufficiency by appealing either to a version of property-instances—and violating One Over Many; or by appealing to a version of aggregates of property-instances—and violating Robustness. In either case, what serve as *truthmakers* are *not universals*, properly so-called—are not, that is, the sorts of things (or somehows) which underlie the manifest fact of Recurrence.

I conclude that an appeal to second-order quantification completely fails to resolve the Fox paradox in any way which reconciles truthmakers with recurrences. The moral remains: that *universals must not be expected to play any distinctive sort of role in truthmaking*.

The converse moral is: that truthmakers must not be expected to be universals in the sense of recurrences. And that leaves an intriguing possibility which is well worth exploring. We might try to construe the subject-matter of mathematics, *not* in terms of recurrence-universals, *but rather*, in terms of the sorts of truthmakers which second-order quantification supplies. Strategies of that general sort have been pursued by Bostock (1974, 1979), and Wright (1983).

If I were unhappy with recurrence-universals, or if I badly wanted mathematics to be as a priori as logic (whatever *that* amounts to!), then I would explore such strategies with more fervour. However, I am untempted by nominalism. And the necessity and a priori status of logic seems to me no less mysterious than that of mathematics; indeed, as I see it, logic has such status only in virtue of being one *branch* of mathematics. Indeed, the closer one gets to logic, and, worse yet, to semantics, the more intractable become the paradoxes and antinomies which confront us. Reducing mathematics to logic seems more to undermine than to ground it. And the same applies to second-order logic. Second-order logic may provide the most satisfying account of truthmakers, but I do not recommend it as providing the subject-matter of mathematics. Mathematics is the theory of universals; and universals must be cut free from any distinctive role in truthmaking. The problems concerning Truthmaker, and the associated logical and set-theoretical paradoxes, are serious problems in their own right. But as Gödel said, in 'What is Cantor's Continuum Problem?' (see Benacerraf and Putnam, 1983, p. 474), 'They are a very serious problem, not for mathematics, however, but rather for logic and epistemology.'

27   Platonism and Necessity

WHAT reasons are there for recognizing the existence of universals? If you reject the Truthmaker axiom, this removes one potent source for theories of universals. Yet if, on the other hand, you accept the Truthmaker axiom, this by itself still provides no good reason for recognizing universals in the recurrence sense. The things which satisfy Truthmaker will be property-instances, or facts, or else they will be higher-order counterparts of these in a hierarchy of logical types. But they will not be things which meet One Over Many and Robustness—they will not be universals. And they will not be the things which furnish the subject-matter of mathematics.

And so we may ask, *do* we need to recognize universals, things which can be wholly present in different regions at the same time, in addition to the stolid middle-sized dry-goods which occupy just one place at a time?

The answer is, yes we do. We do not need recurrence-universals for Truthmaker, or to solve the problem of predication. Why do we need them? Because they are there! We need them if we want a complete picture of what there is, simply because it so happens that *there are* such things. Why do we need echidnas in our theory of the world? Because there are echidnas in the world. And the same goes for universals.

In speaking this way, I am being deliberately obtuse over one sort of problem in order to drive a different point home. I acknowledge, however, that there is a legitimate epistemological question about what *grounds* I have for my assertion that there are universals.

This epistemological question is very hard to answer. But then epistemological questions are often very hard to answer. What grounds do I have for believing in echidnas? I know people who say they have seen some. I have myself seen what I take to have been one, in the wild, as well as several things labelled 'echidna' in the zoo. Yet we have all seen recurrences, too. You may well be uneasy about what 'seeing recurrences' really amounts to, and what sort of justification it really provides for a realist theory of universals. But then equally a good epistemologist can quickly make you uneasy about what the parallel claim amounts to, that someone has 'seen echidnas', and about whether this is a good enough reason for claiming to know there are echidnas.

It is tempting these days for a philosopher to retreat from epistemological questions, and to take refuge in a Popperian sort of scepticism, saying we never really know anything, but that our theory is nevertheless as yet unfalsified, and so worthy of further testing. Or, we may be tempted to fall back on some sort of epistemological *holism*, of a sort we have learned from Quine (1953).

Epistemological holism will console us with the suggestion that, to decide whether something is true, what we must do is to begin with our total web of belief, to try out various alterations, and to change the web only when we find an alteration which counts as an overall improvement. Personally, I am not altogether happy with this picture. But in the absence of anything better, I would urge that, from the perspective of total theory, it does *pay* to acknowledge the existence of universals. Mathematics, properly construed, does commit us to universals; and as yet no alteration to our web of belief which eliminates (or reconstrues) mathematics counts as an overall improvement.

I claim this here without defence, not to persuade, but to clarify just what I am and am not saying about universals. In cutting universals away from truthmakers, I am making their existence a matter, not for a priori proof from logic alone, but for total science. This makes their existence seem in some sense *contingent*; and it becomes a problem for me to explain the apparent *necessity* of mathematical truths. More on this later.

I am not altogether comfortable with holism. In epistemology, my tastes run rather more towards *causal* theories of knowledge.

Causal theories tell us that, in order to know about something, there must be some sort of appropriate causal network linking you with that thing.

Such a theory of knowledge has been perceived by some to be a threat to realist theories of universals, and in particular, a threat to a realist stand on the existence of mathematical entities like numbers. Any yet the causal theory of knowledge should pose no threat to the particular brand of realism I am advocating. It may threaten some brands of 'Platonism'; but it does not threaten my 'Pythagoreanism'. On the view I am urging, there is no reason at all to think that universals are causally isolated from us. It is for that reason that I urge that mathematics is the theory of '*universals*', rather than of 'abstract entities'. The term 'universals' carries the misleading suggestion that I am concerned with truthmakers. But the term 'abstract entities' carries the still more misleading connotation of causal impotence. Universals, if there are any, will be just as causally active as individuals.

And so, if challenged by the question how I *know* there are universals, I am tempted to answer by saying that I 'know' it because my belief in universals *has* been caused in an appropriate way *by universals*—I have seen them, felt them, heard them, ... Such an answer would, of course, be something of a cheat. When asked *how* I know, I am being asked, not for my theory of what knowledge consists in, but for my grounds or justifications for believing what I do. Taken thus, I suppose the question of how I know will drive me back to some sort of holism.

The sceptical question, how we know there are *any* universals, is therefore one which I will largely ignore. The much more productive question to ask, however, is: *how many universals are there?*

If theories if universals are arranged in order of their generosity, according to the number and variety of universals they promise to give us, then the term *Platonism* is generally reserved for *the most generous theories of all*. (As I have been using the term 'Platonism' up until this point, it has covered the full scale of theories which posit recurrences; I am now restricting it to one end of the scale.)

Platonism generally begins from the bold and generous conjecture that *whenever there is somehow that certain things are, then there is something to which those things are related*. From

$$\exists \phi . \phi(a, b, \ldots)$$
(There is somehow that these things are.)

the Platonist infers

$$\exists y \exists \psi . \psi(y, a, b, \ldots)$$
(There is something such that, there is somehow that these things stand to it.)

The Platonist infers a 'something' from every 'somehow'. This is rather closely related to the way a mathematician infers a 'something', a *function*, from any truth of the form '$f(a) = b$'.

In set theory, this bold Platonist conjecture takes the form of the so-called axiom of *comprehension* or *abstraction*—the axiom according to which for any open sentence, ϕx, with free variable x, there will be a set containing all and only the things which satisfy that open sentence.

$$\exists y \forall x . (x \varepsilon y \text{ iff } \phi x).$$

Yet this principle is, notoriously, inconsistent. Its inconsistency can be demonstrated most simply by Russell ((1903), especially chapter 10, on 'The Contradiction'). The contradiction emerges as follows.

Call a set *extroverted* just in case it is not a member of itself. The axiom of abstraction

$$\exists\, y\, \forall\, x.(x\varepsilon y \text{ iff } \phi x)$$

is supposed to be true *whatever* the open sentence ϕx should be; so in particular, it should be true when ϕx is

extroverted(x).

(Being extroverted is a *somehow* that various things are; so there should be a set containing everything that is that now.) And so

$$\exists\, y\, \forall\, x.(x\varepsilon y \text{ iff extroverted}(x)).$$

And yet if there is a set containing all and only extroverted sets, then let us call it R ('the Russell set'). This set will be such that

$$\forall\, x.(x\varepsilon R \text{ iff extroverted}(x)).$$

But this last is a universal generalization; and if true, then what it claims to hold 'for all x' would have to be true of everything *including* R. And that means, it would have to be true that

RεR iff extroverted(R); which is to say,
RεR iff not (RεR).

Yet this is a contradiction. The axiom of abstraction entails a contradiction; and hence it is false.

Russell's paradox undermines any Platonist theory which infers a 'something' from *every* 'somehow'.

This reinforces a moral which I have already drawn from the Fox paradox: universals have nothing special to do with truth. Mathematics is the theory of universals; logic is the theory of truth. So mathematics is not a branch of logic.

That is to say, the existence of the objects of mathematics, like numbers, does not follow from logic alone.

All that remains is the conviction that for at least *some* 'somehows' there are corresponding 'somethings', in the sense of recurrences. And some, perhaps all, of these constitute the subject-matter of mathematics. Yet the question of *which* 'somehows' generate 'somethings' remains an open one: not to be answered by appeal to any a priori principle like Truthmaker or the comprehension axiom.

This would seem to suggest that the truths of mathematics are not after all logically necessary. It suggests that they are contingent: their truth is contingent on the existence of objects, whose existence is not guaranteed by logic alone.

And yet it has been traditional to treat mathematical truths as being necessary in the strongest possible sense: as being true in all possible worlds. My Pythagorean theory needs to account for the high degree of necessity which appears to attach to mathematical truths.

A Quinean stance is open to me here. I could trace the appearance of necessity in mathematics to the depth to which mathematical truths are embedded in our overall theory of the world.

And yet there is more to mathematical necessity than that view allows; or so I believe. One source of the apparent necessity of mathematics is, I suggest, the degree to which the existence of *universals* is independent of the existence of any *particular* collection of objects which instantiate them. And this independence reaches a still greater pitch when the universals we are dealing with instantiate one another. Numbers, for instance, can be numbered. Mathematical patterns themselves instantiate mathematical patterns. That is why pure mathematics is so independent of the world of particulars around us. And that is why mathematical truths seem not to be contingent.

This may not generate the sort of utterly unconditional necessity and a priori certainty which have traditionally been ascribed to mathematics. Yet that sort of necessity or certainty is too much to ask. Mathematical properties and relations instantiate one another; and that makes truths about them largely independent of the world of changing individuals. This independence is what underlies their air of necessity and certainty; it provides them with all the necessity and certainty they are going to get. And that will have to be enough.

ooo : xxx :: xxx : ooo

Bibliography

Aleksandrov, A. D., Kolmogorov, A. N., and Lavent'ev, M. A. (eds.) (1963). *Mathematics: Its Content, Methods, and Meaning*, trans. by S. H. Gould and T. Bartha (MIT Press, Cambridge, Mass.).

Allen, R. D. (1969). 'Individual Properties in Aristotle's Categories', *Phronesis*, 14, 31–9.

Alston, W. P., and Bennett, J. F. (1984). 'Identity and Cardinality: Geach and Frege', *Philosophical Review*, 93, 553–67.

Anscombe, G. E. M. (1981). *Collected Philosophical Papers*, vol. 1: *From Parmenides to Wittgenstein* (Blackwell, Oxford).

Armstrong, D. M. (ed.) (1965). *Berkeley's Philosophical Writings* (Collier, New York).

—— (1978). *Universals and Scientific Realism* (2 vols., CUP, London).

—— (1980a). 'Against "Ostrich" Nominalism. A Reply to Michael Devitt', *Pacific Philosophical Quarterly*, 61, 440–9.

—— (1980b). 'Identity through Time', in P. van Inwagen (ed.), *Time and Cause* (Reidel, Dordrecht).

Austin, J. L. (1968). Trans. of G. Frege, *The Foundations of Arithmetic* (2nd edn., Northwestern, Evanston, Ill.).

Bar-Hillel, Y., Poznanski, E., Rabin, M., and Robinson, A. (1962). *Essays on the Foundations of Mathematics* (North-Holland, Amsterdam).

Barker, S. (1964). *Philosophy of Mathematics* (Prentice-Hall, Englewood Cliffs, NJ).

Bealer, G. (1982). *Quality and Concept* (OUP, New York).

Becker, O. (1936). 'Die Lehre vom Geraden und Ungeraden im neunten Buch der Euklidischen Elemente', *Quellen und Studien zur Geschichte der Mathematik, Astronomie und Physik, B: Studien 3*, 533–53.

—— (1957). *Das Mathematische Denken der Antike* (Vandenhoek & Ruprecht, Göttingen).

Bell, E. T. (1940). *The Development of Mathematics* (McGraw-Hill, London and New York).

—— (1951). *Mathematics: Queen and Servant of Science* (McGraw-Hill, London and New York).

Bell, J. S. (1965). 'On the Einstein, Podolsky, Rosen Paradox', *Physics*, 1, 195–200.

—— (1966). 'On the Problem of Hidden Variables in Quantum Mechanics', *Reviews of Modern Physics*, 38, 447–52.

Benacerraf, P. (1965). 'What Numbers Could Not Be', *Philosophical Review*, 74, 47–73.

—— (1973). 'Mathematical Truth', *Journal of Philosophy*, 70, 661–79.

Benacerraf, P., and Putnam, H. (eds.) (1983). *Philosophy of Mathematics: Selected Readings* (2nd edn., CUP, Cambridge).

Beth, E. W. (1965). *Mathematical Thought: An Introduction to the Philosophy of Mathematics* (Reidel, Dordrecht).

Birch, T. (ed.) (1772). *The Works of the Honourable Robert Boyle* (London; reprinted in part by B. Barger, Sheffield Press, Manhattan Beach, Calif., 1776).

Black, M. (1971). 'The Elusiveness of Sets', *Review of Metaphysics*, 24, 614–36.

Blumenthal, L. (1961). *A Modern View of Geometry* (Dover, New York).

Boehner, P. (1957). Trans. of William of Orkham, *Philosophical Writings: A Selection* (Nelson, London).

Boolos, G. (1971). 'The Iterative Conception of Set', *Journal of Philosophy*, 68, 215–31; reprinted in Benacerraf and Putnam (1983), 486–502.

——(1975). 'On Second-order Logic', *Journal of Philosophy*, 72, 509–27.

——(1984). 'To Be Is to Be a Value of a Variable (or to Be Some Values of Some Variables)', *Journal of Philosophy*, 81, 430–49.

Borst, C. V. (1970). *The Mind-Brain Identity Theory* (Macmillan, London).

Bostock, D. (1974). *Logic and Arithmetic: Natural Numbers* (Clarendon Press, Oxford).

——(1979). *Logic and Arithmetic: Rational and Irrational Numbers* (Clarendon Press, Oxford).

Bourbaki, N. (1968). *Elements of Mathematics: Theory of Sets* (Hermann, Paris).

Boyer, C. B. (1968). *A History of Mathematics* (Wiley, New York, Sydney, and London).

Bradley, F. H. (1893). *Appearance and Reality* (OUP, Oxford; reprinted in paperback, 1969).

Brouwer, L. E. J. (1981). *Brouwer's Cambridge Lectures on Intuitionism*, ed. D. van Dalen (CUP, London and New York).

Browder, F., and MacLane, S. (1978). 'The Relevance of Mathematics', in L. Steen (ed), *Mathematics Today* (Springer-Verlay, Berlin), 323–49.

Burgess, J. P. (1983). 'Why I Am Not a Nominalist', *Notre Dame Journal of Formal Logic*, 24, 93–105.

Burkert, W. (1972). *Lore and Science in Ancient Pythagoreanism*, trans. by E. L. Minar jun. (Harvard University Press, Cambridge, Mass.).

Campbell, K. (1970). *Body and Mind* (Doubleday, New York).

——(1976). *Metaphysics: An Introduction* (Dickenson, Encino, Calif.).

Cantor, G. (1895). 'Beitrage zur Begrundung der transfiniten Mengenlehre, I', *Mathematische Annalen* 46. English trans. by P. E. B. Jourdain, *Contributions to the Founding of the Theory of Transfinite Numbers* (Dover, New York, 1915 and 1955).

Chihara, C. S. (1968). 'Our Ontological Commitment to Universals', *Noûs*, 2, 25–46.

—— (1973). *Ontology and the Vicious-Circle Principle* (Cornell University Press, Ithaca, NY).

—— (1982). 'A Gödelian Thesis regarding Mathematic Objects: Do They Exist? And Can We Perceive Them?' *Philosophical Review*, 91, 211–27.

Chisholm, R. M. (1973). 'Parts as Essential to Their Wholes', *Review of Metaphysics*, 26, 581–603.

Cochiarella, N. (1980). 'Nominalism and Conceptualism as Predicative Second-order Theories of Predication', *Notre Dame Journal of Formal Logic*, 21, 481–500.

Cohen, P. J. (1966). *Set Theory and the Continuum Hypothesis* (Benjamin, Reading, Mass.).

Courant, R., and Robbins, H. (1941). *What Is Mathematics? An Elementary Approach to Ideas and Methods* (OUP, London and New York; reprinted 1969).

Cranston, M. (ed.) (1965). *Locke's Essay Concerning Human Understanding* (Collier, New York).

Crew, H., and de Salvio, A. (1954). Trans. of Galileo Galilei, *Dialogues Concerning Two New Sciences* (Dover, New York).

Crossley, J. N. (1980). *The Emergence of Number* (Upside Down A Book, Yarra Glen, Victoria).

Currie, G. (1978). 'Frege's Realism', *Inquiry*, 21, 218–21.

—— (1982a). 'Frege, Sense, and Mathematical Knowledge', *Australasian Journal of Philosophy*, 60, 5–19.

—— (1982b). *Frege: An Introduction to his Philosophy* (Harvester, Brighton).

—— (1986). 'Continuity and Change in Frege's Philosophy of Mathematics', in L. Haaparanta and J. Hintikka (eds.), *Frege Synthesized* (Reidel, Dordrecht), 345–73.

Curry, H. B. (1951). *Outlines of a Formalist Philosophy of Mathematics* (North-Holland, Amsterdam).

Dantzig, T. (1954). *Number: The Language of Science; a Critical Survey Written for the Cultured Non-Mathematician* (4th edn., rev., Allen & Unwin, London).

Dedekind, R. (1888). *Was Sind und Was Sollen die Zahlen?* (Brunswick); trans. by W. Beman, *Dedekind's Essays of the Theory of Numbers* (Open Court, New York, 1901; republished, Dover, New York, 1963).

Devitt, M. (1980). '"Ostrich" Nominalism or "Mirage" Realism?', *Pacific Philosophical Quarterly*, 61, 433–9.

Dirac, P. A. M. (1947). *The Principles of Quantum Mechanics* (3rd edn., Clarendon Press, Oxford).

Drake, S., and O'Malley, C. D. (eds.) (1960). *The Controversy on the Comets of 1618* (University of Pennsylvania Press, Philadelphia, Pa.).

Dummett, M. (1973). *Frege: Philosophy of Language* (Duckworth, London; 2nd edn. 1981).

—— (1978). *Elements of Intuitionism* (OUP, Oxford).

Dummett, M. (1981). *The Interpretation of Frege's Philosophy* (Duckworth, London).

—— (1982). 'Realism', *Synthese*, 52, 55–112.

Einstein, A. (1956). *The Meaning of Relativity* (6th edn., rev., Methuen, London).

—— Podolsky, B., and Rosen, N. (1935). 'Can Quantum-Mechanical Description of Physical Reality be Considered Complete?', *Physical Review*, 47, 777–80.

Ellis, B. D. (1966). *Basic Concepts of Measurement* (CUP, London).

Field, H. H. (1980). *Science without Numbers* (Blackwell, Oxford).

Fox, J. F. (1987). 'Truthmaker', *Australasian Journal of Philosophy*, 65, 188–207.

Fraenkel, A. A. (1961). *Abstract Set Theory* (2nd. edn., North-Holland, Amsterdam).

Frege, G. (1893–1903). *Grundgesetze der Arithmetik* (2 vols., Hermann Pohle, Jena; reprinted, Hildesheim, 1962). Parts trans. by M. Furth in *The Basic Laws of Arithmetic* (University of California Press, Berkeley, Calif., 1967).

—— (1979). *Posthumous Writings*, ed. H. Hermes, F. Kambartel, and F. Kaulbach (Blackwell, Oxford).

Fritz, K. von (1945). 'The Discovery of the Incommensurables by Hippasos of Metapositum', *Annals of Mathematics*, 46, 242–64.

Geach, P., and Black, M. (1970). *Translations from the Philosophical Writings of Gottlob Frege* (Blackwell, Oxford).

Gerhardt, C. I. (ed.) (1899). *Der Briefwechsel von Gottfried Wilhelm Leibniz mit Mathemtikern* (Berlin). Cited in Crossley (1980).

Gödel, K. (1944). 'Russell's Mathematical Logic', in P. A. Schilpp (ed.), *The Philosophy of Bertrand Russell* (CUP, Cambridge). Reprinted in Benacerraf and Putnam (1983), 447–69.

—— (1947). 'What Is Cantor's Continuum Problem?' *American Mathematical Monthly*, 54, 515–25; rev. and expanded version in Benacerraf and Putnam (1983), 470–86.

Goldman, A. I. (1967). 'A Causal Theory of Knowing', *Journal of Philosophy* 64, 357–72.

Goodman, N. (1966). *The Structure of Appearance* (2nd edn., Harvard University Press, Cambridge, Mass.).

—— and Leonard, H. (1940). 'The Calculus of Individuals and Its Uses', *Journal of Symbolic Logic*, 5, 45–55.

—— and Quine, W. V. (1947). 'Steps toward a Constructive Nominalism', *Journal of Symbolic Logic*, 12, 105–22.

Goodman, N. D. (1979). 'Mathematics as an Objective Science', *American Mathematical Monthly*, 86, 540–55.

Gottlieb, D. (1978). 'The Truth about Arithmetic', *American Philosophical Quarterly*, 15, 81–90.

Grandy, R. E. (1976). 'Anadic Logic and English', *Synthese*, 32, 395–402.

—— (1977a). 'In Defense of a Modest Platonism', *Philosophical Studies*, 32, 359–69.

—— (1977b). *Advanced Logic for Applications* (Reidel, Dordrecht).

Grattan-Guinness, I. (ed.) (1970). *The Development of the Foundation of Analysis from Euler to Riemann* (MIT Press, Cambridge, Mass.).

Haldane, E. S., and Ross, G. R. T. (1970). Trans. of *The Philosophical Works of Descartes* (CUP, Cambridge).

Halmos, P. R. (1960). *Naïve Set Theory* (Van Nostrand, London and New York).

Hambourger, R. (1977). 'A Difficulty with the Frege–Russell Definition of Number', *Journal of Philosophy*, 74, 409–14.

Hamming, R. W. (1980). 'The Unreasonable Effectiveness of Mathematics', *American Mathematical Monthly*, 87, 81–90.

Hardy, G. H. (1940). *A Mathematician's Apology* (Macmillan, New York).

—— and Wright E. M. (1938). *An Introduction to the Theory of Numbers* (OUP, Oxford; 4th edn., 1960).

Hazen, A. (1985). Review of C. Wright, *Frege's Conception of Numbers as Objects*, *Australasian Journal of Philosophy*, 63, 251–4.

Heath, T. L. (ed.) (1897). *The Works of Archimedes* (Dover, New York; reissued with a supplement, *The Method of Archimedes*, 1972).

—— (1921). *A History of Greek Mathematics: I. From Thales to Euclid* (OUP, Oxford).

Heiberg, J. L., and Menge, H. (eds.) (1883–1916). *Euclid's Opera Omnia* (10 vols., Leipzig). Trans. by T. L. Heath, *Euclid's Element* (Dover, New York, 1956).

Hempel, C. G. (1945a). 'Geometry and Empirical Science', *American Mathematical Monthly*, 52, 7–17.

—— (1945b). 'On the Nature of Mathematical Truth', *American Mathematical Monthly*, 52, 543–56; reprinted in Benacerraf and Putnam (1964), 258–73.

Hewlett, J. (1822). Trans. of L. Euler, *Elements of Algebra* (3rd edn., J. Jonson & Co., London).

Heyting, A. (1956). *Intuitionism: An Introduction* (North-Holland, Amsterdam).

Heywood, R. B. (ed.), (1947). *The Works of the Mind* (University of Chicago Press, Chicago, Ill.).

Hilbert, D., and Bernays, P. (1971). *Foundations of Geometry*, trans. by L. Unger (2nd edn., Open Court, La Salle, Ill.).

—— and Ackerman, W. (1928). *Principles of Mathematical Logic* (Chelsea, New York).

Hintikka, J. (1969). *The Philosophy of Mathematics* (CUP, London).

Hiriyanna, M. (1932). *Outlines of Indian Philosophy* (Allen & Unwin, London).

Jones, D. E., and Walley, J. T. (1899). Trans. of H. Hertz, *The Principles of Mechanics, Presented in a New Form* (Macmillan, London).

Jubien, M. (1977). 'Ontology and Mathematical Truth', *Noûs*, 11, 133–50.

Kasner, E., and Newman, J. (1968). *Mathematics and the Imagination* (Penguin, Harmondsworth).

Kelley, J. L. (1955). *General Topology* (Van Nostrand, New York).

Kessler, G. (1980). 'Frege, Mill, and the Foundations of Arithmetic', *Journal of Philosophy*, 77, 65–79.

Kim, J. (1981). 'The Role of Perception in *a priori* Knowledge: Some Remarks', *Philosophical Studies*, 40, 339–54.

——(1982). 'Perceiving Numbers and Numerical Relations', *Noûs*, 16, 93–4.

Kirk, G. S., and Raven, J. E. (1957). *The Presocratic Philosophers* (CUP, London).

Kitcher, P. (1978). 'The Plight of the Platonist', *Noûs*, 12, 119–36.

——(1980). 'Arithmetic for the Millian', *Philosophical Studies* 37, 215–36.

——(1983). *The Nature of Mathematical Knowledge* (OUP, Oxford).

Kluge, E.-H. W. (1971). Trans. of G. W. Frege, *On the Foundations of Geometry and Formal Theories of Arithmetic* (Yale University Press, New Haven, Conn., and London).

Körner, S. (1960). *The Philosophy of Mathematics* (Hutchinson, London).

Lakatos, I. (1976). *Proofs and Refutations*, ed. J. Warroll and E. Zahar (CUP, London).

Lambros, C. H. (1976). 'Are Numbers Properties of Objects?' *Philosophical Studies*, 29, 381–9.

Lasserre, F. (1964). *The Birth of Mathematics in the Age of Plato* (Meridian Books, Cleveland, Ohio and New York).

Lear, J. (1977). 'Sets and Semantics', *Journal of Philosophy*, 74, 86–102.

——(1982). 'Aristotle's Philosophy of Mathematics', *Philosophical Review*, 91, 161–92.

Lebesgue, H. L. (1966). *Measure and the Integral*, ed. K. O. May (Holden-Day, San Francisco, Calif.).

Lehman, H. (1979). *Introduction to the Philosophy of Mathematics* (Blackwell, Oxford).

Lemmon, E. J. (1969). *Introduction to Axiomatic Set Theory* (Routledge & Kegan Paul, London).

Lewis, D. K. (1968). 'Counterpart Theory and Quantified Modal Logic', *Journal of Philosophy*, 65, 113–26.

——(1983). 'New Work for a Theory of Universals', *Australasian Journal of Philosophy*, 61, 343–77.

——(1986). *On the Plurality of Worlds* (Blackwell, Oxford).

Loux, M. J. (1970). *Universals and Particulars: Readings in Ontology* (Anchor, New York).

——(1974). *Ockham's Theory of Terms* (University of Notre Dame Press, Notre Dame, Ind.).

—— (1978). *Substance and Attribute: A Study in Ontology* (Reidel, Dordrecht).

Lucas, P. G., and Grint, L. (1953). Trans. of G. W. Leibniz, *Discourse on Metaphysics* (Manchester University Press, Manchester), sect. xxx.

MacLane, S. (1981). 'Mathematical Models: A Sketch for the Philosophy of Mathematics', *American Mathematical Monthly*, 88, 462–72.

—— (1980). 'Mathematical Models of Space', *American Scientist*, 68, 184–91.

Maddy, P. (1980). 'Perception and Mathematical Intuition', *Philosophical Review*, 89, 163–96.

—— (1981). 'Sets and Numbers', *Noûs*, 15, 495–511.

—— (1982). 'Mathematical Epistemology: What Is the Question?', *Noûs*, 16, 106–7.

—— (1983). 'Proper Classes', *Journal of Symbolic Logic*, 48, 113–39.

Minogue, B. P. (1977). 'Numbers, Properties, and Frege', *Philosophical Studies*, 31, 423–7.

Morse, A. P. (1965). *A Theory of Sets* (Academic Press, New York).

Morton, A. (1975). 'Complex Individuals and Multigrade Relations', *Noûs*, 9, 309–18.

Mulligan, K., Simons, P., and Smith, B. (1984). 'Truth-Makers', *Philosophy and Phenomenological Research*, 44, 287–321.

Munro, H. A. J. (1965). Trans. of Lucretius, *On the Nature of Things* (Washington Square, New York).

Nelson, T. M., and Bartley, S. H. (1961). 'Numerosity, Number, Arithmetization, and Psychology', *Philosophy of Science*, 28, 178–203.

Neumann, J. von (1947). 'The Mathematician', reprinted in Heywood (1947), 180–96.

Newton, I. (1728). *Arithmetica Universalis* (2nd edn., Longman, London).

—— (1730). *Opticks* (4th edn., W. & J. Innys, London; reprinted, Dover, New York, 1952).

Oldfield, E. (1981). 'Reference to Abstract Entities', *Canadian Journal of Philosophy*, 11, 425–38.

Ore, Ø. (1953). *Cardano, The Gamboling Scholar* (Princeton University Press, Princeton, NJ).

Parsons, C. (1974). 'Sets and Classes', *Noûs*, 8, 7–9.

—— (1977). 'What is the Iterative Conception of Set?' in *Logic, Foundations of Mathematics and Computability Theory*, ed. R. E. Butts and J. Hintikka (Reidel, Dordrecht), 335–7; reprinted in Benacerraf and Putnam (1983), 503–29.

Pears, D. (ed.) (1972). *Russell's Logical Atomism* (Fontana, London).

Poincaré, H. (1905). *Science and Hypothesis* (Walter Scott Publ. Co.; reprinted Dover, New York, 1952).

Polya, G. (1945). *How to Solve It: A New Aspect of Mathematical Method* (Princeton University Press, Princeton, NJ).

—— (1954). *Induction and Analogy in Mathematics* (Princeton University Press, Princeton, NJ).

Popper, K. R. (1959). *The Logic of Scientific Discovery* (Hutchinson, London; rev. edn., 1969).

Price, H. H. (1962). *Thinking and Experience* (Harvard University Press, Cambridge, Mass.).

Prior, A. N. (1955). *Formal Logic* (Clarendon Press, Oxford).

Putnam, H. (1971). *Philosophy of Logic* (Harper & Row, New York).

——(1979). *Philosophical Papers, 2: Mathematics, Matter and Method* (2nd edn., CUP, London).

Quine, W. V. (1941). 'Whitehead and the Rise of Modern Logic', in P. A. Schilpp (ed.), *The Philosophy of Alfred North Whitehead* (Open Court, La Salle, Ill.), 125–63.

——(1953). *From a Logical Point of View* (Harvard University Press, Cambridge, Mass.; 2nd edn., rev. Harper & Row, New York, 1961).

——(1964). 'Ontological Reduction and the World of Numbers', *Journal of Philosophy*, 61; reprinted with changes in *The Ways of Paradox and Other Essays* (Random House, New York, 1966), 199–207.

——(1969). *Set Theory and Its Logic* (rev. edn., Harvard University Press, Cambridge, Mass.).

——(1980). 'Soft Impeachment Disowned', *Pacific Philosophical Quarterly*, 61, 450–1.

Ramsey, F. P. (1929). 'Mathematics, Foundations of' in *Encyclopaedia Britannica*, vol. 15 (14th edn., London and New York), 82–4.

——(1931). *The Foundations of Mathematics and Other Logical Essays*, ed. R. B. Braithwaite (Routledge & Kegan Paul, London).

Resnik, M. D. (1965). 'Frege's Theory of Incomplete Entities', *Philosophy of Science*, 32, 329–41.

——(1975). 'Mathematical Knowledge and Pattern Recognition', *Canadian Journal of Philosophy*, 5, 25–39.

——(1980). *Frege and the Philosophy of Mathematics* (Cornell University Press, Ithaca, NY, and London).

——(1981). 'Mathematics as a Science of Patterns: Ontology and Reference', *Noûs*, 15, 529–50.

——(1982). 'Mathematics as a Science of Patterns: Epistemology', *Noûs*, 16, 95–105.

Robinson, D. (1982). 'Re-identifying Matter', *Philosophical Review*, 91, 317–41.

Robson, J. M. (ed) (1973). J. S. Mill's *A System of Logic* (Routledge & Kegan Paul, London).

Ross, W. D. (ed) (1928). *The Works of Aristotle*, vol. 8: *Metaphysica* (2nd edn., Clarendon Press, Oxford).

Russell, B. (1903). *The Principles of Mathematics* (Norton, New York).

——(1912). *The Problems of Philosophy* (Home University Library; reprinted, OUP, Oxford, 1959).

—— (1919). *An Introduction to Mathematical Philosophy* (Allen & Unwin, London, and Macmillan, New York).

—— (1956). *Logic and Knowledge: Essays 1901–1950*, ed. R. C. Marsh (Allen & Unwin, London).

Sawyer, W. W. (1943). *Mathematician's Delight* (Penguin, London).

Scott, D. (1962). 'More on the Axiom of Extensionality' in Bar-Hillel *et al.* (1962), 115–31.

Selby-Bigge, L. A. (ed.) (1960). Hume's *A Treatise on Human Nature* (Clarendon Press, Oxford).

Sellars, W. (1963). 'Abstract Entities', *Review of Metaphysics*, 16, 627–71.

Shapiro, S. (1983). 'Mathematics and Reality', *Philosophy of Science*, 50, 523–48.

Sharvey, R. (1968). 'Why a Class Can't Change Its Members', *Noûs*, 2, 303–14.

—— (1980). 'A More General Theory of Definite Descriptions', *Philosophical Review*, 89, 607–24.

Shimony, A. (1963). 'The Role of the Observer in Quantum Theory', *American Journal of Physics*, 31, 755–73.

Simons, P. M. (1980). 'Individuals, Groups and Manifolds' in R. Haller and W. Grassl (eds.), *Language, Logic, and Philosophy: Proceedings of the 4th International Wittgenstein Symposium* (Holder-Pichler-Tempsky, Vienna), 483–6.

—— (1982). 'Against the Aggregate Theory of Number', *Journal of Philosophy*, 79, 163–7.

Smeltzer, D. (1970). *Man and Number: An Account of the Development of Man's Use of Number through the Ages* (A. & C. Black, London).

Smith, D. E. (ed.) (1929). *A Source Book in Mathematics* (McGraw-Hill, London and New York).

—— and Latham, M. L. (1925). Trans. of *The Geometry of René Descartes* (Open Court, Chicago and London).

Snapper, E. (1979). 'What Is Mathematics?' *American Mathematical Monthly*, 86, 551–7.

Stcherbatsky, F. Th. (1962). *Buddhist Logic*, vol. 2 (Dover, New York).

Steiner, M. (1975). *Mathematical Knowledge* (Cornell Univesity Press, Ithaca, NY, and London).

—— (1978). 'Mathematics, Explanation, and Scientific Knowledge', *Noûs*, 12, 17–28.

—— (1983). 'Mathematical Realism', *Noûs*, 17, 363–85.

Stenius, E. (1974). 'Sets', *Synthese*, 27, 161–88.

Stout, G. F. (1921). *On the Nature of Universals and Propositions* (British Academy Lecture; OUP, Oxford), reprinted in G. F. Stout, *Studies in Philosophy and Psychology* (Macmillan, London, 1930), 384–403.

Strawson, P. F. (1959). *Individuals: An Essay in Descriptive Metaphysics* (Methuen, London).

Struik, D. J. (1969). *A Source Book in Mathematics: 1200–1800* (Harvard University Press, Cambridge, Mass.).

Tarski, A. (1956). *Logic, Semantics, Mathematics* (OUP, Oxford).

Vaihinger, H. (1924). *The Philosophy of 'As If'*, trans. C. K. Ogden (Kegan Paul, Trench, Trubner & Co., London; Harcourt, Brace & Co., New York).

Waerden, van der, B. L. (1954). *Science Awakening: Egyptian, Babylonian and Greek Mathematics*, trans. by A. Dresden (Noordhoff, Gröningen; and Science Editions, New York, 1961).

Wagner, S. (1982). 'Arithmetical Fiction', *Pacific Philosophical Quarterly*, 63, 255–69.

Wang, H. (1974). *From Mathematics to Philosophy* (Humanities Press, New York).

Weyl, H. (1949). *Philosophy of Mathematics and Natural Science* (Princeton University Press, Princeton, NJ).

White, N. P. (1974). 'What Numbers Are', *Synthese*, 27, 111–24.

Whitehead, A. N. and Russell, B. (1910–13). *Principia Mathematica* (CUP, Cambridge; 2nd edn. 1925–7).

Wiener, N. (1912–14). 'A Simplification of the Logic of Relations', *Proceedings of the Cambridge Philosophical Society* 17, 387–90; reprinted in Heijenoort (1967).

Wigner, E. P. (1960). 'The Unreasonable Effectiveness of Mathematics in the Natural Sciences', *Communications in Pure and Applied Mathematics*, 13; reprinted in E. P. Wigner, *Symmetries and Reflections* (Indiana University Press, Bloomington, Ind., and London, 1967), 222–37.

Wilder, R. L. (1975). *Evolution of Mathematical Concepts* (Wiley, New York).

Williams, D. C. (1953). 'On the Elements of Being: I', *Review of Metaphysics*, 7, 3–18.

—— (1986). 'Universals and Existents', *Australasian Journal of Philosophy*, 64, 1–14.

Witmer, T. R. (1968). Trans. of G. Cardano, *The Great Art, or Rules of Algebra* (MIT Press, Cambridge, Mass.).

Wittgenstein, L. (1922). *Tractatus Logico-Philosophicus*, trans. D. E. Pears and B. F. McGuinness (Routledge & Kegan Paul, London).

—— (1956a). *Remarks on the Foundations of Mathematics*, trans. G. E. M. Anscombe (Blackwell, Oxford).

—— (1956b). *Philosophical Investigations*, trans. G. E. M. Anscombe (Blackwell, Oxford).

Wright, C. (1983). *Frege's Theory of Numbers as Objects* (Aberdeen University Press, Aberdeen).

Young, W. H., and Young, G. C. (1906). *The Theory of Sets of Points* (CUP, Cambridge).

INDEX